Praise for

Notes From Breakfast Creek
A Look at the World

"Reading Cathy Salter's prose from Breakfast Creek is like breathing the spring air. Or should I say the fall air? Why don't I say both the spring and the fall air, because—among other virtues—this is a book for all seasons. Salter mixes intellect, emotion and description about rural life, with a bonus of contrasting it to urban life for those of us unable to move to the country."

—Steve Weinberg, author of *Taking on the Trust: The Epic Battle of Ida Tarbell and John D. Rockefeller*, and *Armand Hammer: The Untold Story*.

✣ ✣ ✣

"Cathy Salter had a dream of home. In the ripeness of years, she and her husband, Kit, lived that dream in an old stone house in the farmland woods of central Missouri, in a place they called Breakfast Creek. This book invites the reader to share walks in the wild places, to feel life rising in warm bread dough, and to raise a glass of wine over lazy talk before a hearth fire on a chill day. Readers will love the silky prose of this heartfelt tribute to the well-lived life."

—Jane Duncan Flink, author of *Unmarked Trails* and past Editor of the *Boone County Journal*.

✣ ✣ ✣

"Reading [Cathy Salter's] essays is akin to snuggling into a warm bed on a cold night and awaking refreshed."

—Grady Clay, author of *Close-Up, Right Before Your Eyes*, *Crossing the American Grain*, and past editor of *Landscape Architecture*.

✣ ✣ ✣

Notes From Breakfast Creek

Cathy Salter

For Kit, who completes my world.
Near and far, now and forever....

Notes From Breakfast Creek

A Look at the World

Cathy Salter

iUniverse, Inc.
New York Bloomington

Notes From Breakfast Creek
A Look at the World

Copyright © 2008 by Cathy Salter

All rights reserved. No part of this book may be used or reproduced by any means, graphic, electronic, or mechanical, including photocopying, recording, taping or by any information storage retrieval system without the written permission of the publisher except in the case of brief quotations embodied in critical articles and reviews.

iUniverse books may be ordered through booksellers or by contacting:

iUniverse
1663 Liberty Drive
Bloomington, IN 47403
www.iuniverse.com
1-800-Authors (1-800-288-4677)

Because of the dynamic nature of the Internet, any Web addresses or links contained in this book may have changed since publication and may no longer be valid.

The views expressed in this work are solely those of the author and do not necessarily reflect the views of the publisher, and the publisher hereby disclaims any responsibility for them.

ISBN: 978-0-595-52426-6 (pbk)
ISBN: 978-0-595-62480-5 (ebk)

Printed in the United States of America

Life is not measured by the number of breaths we take
but by the places and moments that take our breath away.

Anonymous

Contents

Praise for i

Introduction xiii

Acknowledgements xix

Chapter One

Images of the Rural Scene 1

    Clotheslines 2

    A Farm Auction 4

    Truck Talk at Rice's Garage 7

    Where the River Flowed 9

    Seen from Above 12

    Dancing in the Moonlight 15

    Once in a Blue Moon 18

Chapter Two

The Cycle of Seasons and Elements ... 21

    Spring's Splendid Arrival 22

    Sweet Disorder 25

    Bees' Wings 28

    A Taste of Autumn 31

    Winter's Hard Edge 34

Winter Gatherings 37

Chapter Three

The Animals at Breakfast Creek 39

    A Tree Frog. 40

    Angels in Our Lives 42

    Shades of Gray 45

    Walkabout Time. 48

    Gossamer 51

    Geese and Grass 54

    Ella and the Great Blue Heron 57

    Sam Walker 60

Chapter Four

Gardens. 65

    The Purples of Spring. 66

    May Days 68

    A Teacher's Garden 71

    Maxine. 74

    A Perfect Sunday 78

    Peas and Nature's Palimpsest. 81

Chapter Five

Food and the Kitchen 85

    Sweet Apple Times 86

Hand Made Breads..89

Corn and Tomatoes..92

Comforting Thoughts....................................95

American Pie..98

Garam Masala...101

Chapter Six

Family..105

A Solid Citizen...106

Beginning in 1945..109

Backyards..112

A Wing and a Prayer...................................115

Auctions and Families Past.........................118

The Girls...121

Nicolás..124

Chapter Seven

Cities..127

City Images and the Power of Pruning......128

The Walls of the City Speak.......................131

Celebrating Chicago....................................135

This Thing Called California......................138

Dos Viajaros...141

Ah, Paris!..144

Outrageous Beauty......................................146

Chapter Eight

Other Places 149

    Tangerine 150

    From a Distance 153

    Hands at Work 156

    A Wedding in Milan 159

    Back of Beyond 162

    Roads Taken 165

Chapter Nine

A Writer's Imagination 169

    A Good Pen and a Cup of Coffee 170

    The Girl in the Picture 173

    Quiet Places 176

    The Red Shoes 179

    Travel Across Time 182

    Finding E. B. White 185

    Images of Sand and Saffron 188

    Havana Dreaming 191

    Documenting My Conversation with Denzel 193

Introduction

🌲 On the Naming of Places ...

People have always loved naming places. Over time, the names they attach to certain sites or regions become a record of the people, events, products and geography of that place. Boise, the state capital of Idaho, derives its name from the French *riviere boisee* after the "wooded river" on which it stands. Brazil was named after the red dye (*braza* in Portuguese) gotten from brazil wood. In a French text published in 1688, Chicago was referred to as *Chigagou*, the Algonquian word for "stinking"—probably referring to either the smell of wild onion growing in the area, the smell of stagnant marshland around Lake Michigan, or to skunk whose fur was highly valued at the time. The state of Missouri took its name from a great river that is the longest tributary of the Mississippi River. Like Chicago, Missouri is a word with Native American roots, probably the Dakota word for "muddy" referring to the quantities of silt carried downstream by the river.

Around southern Boone County in the heart of Missouri, street signs with names such as Sapp, Nichols, Bullard, Dusenbery and Lloyd Hudson are a record of the person or family who first lived down that road. Turkey Creek was probably a popular spot seasonally for local wild turkey hunters, or maybe someone gave it that name hoping the other hunters would be drawn there, lessening the field of competition. And on land now managed by the Forest Service, Burnett School Road is still the site of a white, one-room schoolhouse from an earlier era.

Hartsburg, named after local settler A. B. Hart, is a river town whose geography and people inspired many of the stories in this book. It is located at the end of Route A about five miles west of Highway 63. After a final descent down Nichols Hill, the narrow, two-lane road enters town, takes a slight curve, then flows into Second Street—the main artery leading into and out of town. Main Street developed primarily as a residential street, with the exception of the Baptist Church at the corner of Main St. and First. First Street linked early Hartsburg with river access and transportation at Bush Landing on the Missouri River.

The Missouri Kansas Texas Railroad made a diagonal slice through the corner of town where the train's depot, the mill, and the Globe Hotel were located.

Horses were liveried on Main Street, mail was posted and received on Second Street and up to 26 businesses once existed around the three banks that served this farming community over the first half of the 20th century. Residential plots pushed upslope away from the river and the business end of town, out of the river's way until the 500-year flood of 1993. In the past 100 years, Hartsburg has seen changes in transportation as well as shifts in the river's course that must be understood to make sense of the town's orientation today. Families with ties to earlier generations that settled Hartsburg and the nearby town of Ashland still live throughout the area. Their stories to this day can be found on buildings, road signs and in church cemeteries sprinkled throughout the county.

Breakfast Creek's name came from another world, one that my husband, Kit, and I had explored before we knew the first thing about Hartsburg (our postal address in Missouri), Ashland or the world of southern Boone County. To folks native to the area, the house we purchased on Westbrook Drive was the "rock house" built in 1948 by Joe Klupp from native limestone. To others who knew it in the 1970s and '80s, it was the Franklin place. Ralph and Betty Jo Franklin called it Hampton Moors. To Mrs. Loy Martin who wrote a history of our property for a Jones family reunion in 1962, it was the home of Franklin Jones, better known as "Uncle Bob" Jones. At the time of the 1962 Jones family reunion, Uncle Bob was the only remaining first generation descendent of an original Boone County settler—William Mosias Jones—who took a patent on 40 acres of land July 22, 1839. It was on this same place that Uncle Bob was born in 1878. And it was on the original house site on this parcel of land that Bob, a bachelor, still lived with his niece, Mrs. Joe Klupp, and her husband 32 years ago.

When Kit and I arrived on the scene in October 1988, we knew nothing of the prior naming history of this unique property that had been home to Uncle Bob Jones for 76 years. Its pastures and pond were worlds that would not be explored until we had settled into the house and made it our own. A first step in that sense of ownership was finding the right name for it. For months, a name eluded us. Extended family and friends offered seeming endless suggestions—Grey Goose Pond, Walnut Acres, Goose Creek, and so on. Finally, a moratorium was placed on the name search and we focused our energy on growing into our newly purchased seven acres in the country. One day, it just happened. The name "Breakfast Creek" emerged from another world and time in our past. It simply fit, as though it had always belonged to the place.

On the Road …

Breakfast Creek is not a bed and breakfast, and its creek is intermittent. The name comes from a small town founded on a creek not far from Brisbane, Australia. It is also the name of the town's original 19th century tavern that is today a popular restaurant and bar. The name on a road sign caught my attention during a trip to Australia that Kit and I made in August 1988. It was just a name read from the window of an airport taxi on our way into Brisbane. A name about which I knew nothing, that quietly slipped into my mental archive of place memorabilia until I had a reason to retrieve it and learn its story.

Kit and I moved to Missouri in October 1988, and for the next 16 years it remained our base and my anchor point. Our seven acres were located on Westbrook Drive three miles south of the Highway 63 turn-off to Hartsburg and five miles south of Ashland. This gently winding, paved two-lane country road was once part of the old highway connecting Columbia and Missouri's state capital, Jefferson City. Cut off like an oxbow on a meandering river, it wanders as it pleases over and around the area's rich limestone relief.

As we grew into life in the country, Breakfast Creek took on a life of its own. It was a place that was nowhere to be found on any map of Boone County, but in time it became a real place in the minds of family and friends, and readers of Ashland's *Boone County Journal* and later the *Columbia Daily Tribune*. It was there that subscribers read the weekly stories I wrote during the magical years that Kit and I shared life at Breakfast Creek with two docile dogs, a caboodle of cats, paddlings of ducks, a gaggle of nine geese, a solitary blue heron, and multitudes of memorable creatures in the wild that came and went at will. It was there, in my weekly column called "Notes From Breakfast Creek," that the place found its way into the local vocabulary and gradually became a weekly geographic stopping place for my regular readers. To this day, letters are delivered to Breakfast Creek, MO with only the benefit of a zip code to guide them.

In a metaphorical sense, our 1988 move to a small farm in mid-Missouri after more than a decade of teaching geography in urban Los Angeles followed by a two-year assignment at the National Geographic Society in Washington, D.C. represented a fork in the road for me after a 20-year career in teaching. I was suddenly faced with two options—return to teaching or focus my energies on learning about life in the country. My father, a career Air Force officer, had grown up on a dairy farm and something in my genetic makeup told me that if I was ever going to learn the difference between a bale of straw and a bale of hay, this was my chance, sister. Thus, I chose the road less traveled immortalized in Robert Frost's poem, "The Road Not Taken"—

*Two Roads diverged in a wood, and I—
I took the one less traveled by,
And that has made all the difference.*

🖋 On Becoming a Writer ...

For the next 16 years, Breakfast Creek would remain my base from which to view the world, up close and from a distance. It is where, in an effort to follow a path anchored deep within my soul, I set out on a new road filled with possibilities that until then were untested. Writing, it turned out, became my "road less traveled," and it is one I continue to explore.

Every Monday morning, I sit down and look into a blank screen on my computer. Each story begins with a single word. Words collected become threads. Threads are woven together and each story's telling becomes a journey. Each week as I launch off in a new direction, I wonder just where the journey will lead me. That is part of the mystery and allure that comes with writing and with taking the road less traveled.

My first column appeared in Ashland's *Boone County Journal* following the Great Midwestern Flood of 1993. After witnessing the physical and human drama of that 500-year flood as it played out in towns like Hartsburg situated on the Missouri River, I was moved to write. That first story, "Where the River Flowed," led to two others, and finally to a trip to *Boone County Journal* office in Ashland.

I recall walking to the Editor's desk located bulls-eye center in a large room. There Jane Duncan Flink was busily writing an editorial amidst the frenetic goings and comings around her. Gathering up my courage, I marched over and introduced myself to this lovely woman with bright, intelligent eyes. As I mentioned three pieces of my writing that Jane and her husband, Richard Flink, had published over the past several months, she gave me her full attention. "What would you think about the idea of me writing a weekly column for your paper?" I asked. "I'd call it 'Notes From Breakfast Creek'?"

"Let's do it!" Jane agreed enthusiastically, and with that, our friendship and my career as a newspaper columnist took off. I drove home that morning, wondering what in the world I would find to write about given a weekly deadline, but I needn't have worried. For the next twelve years, "Notes From Breakfast Creek" allowed me the space to explore worlds both near and distant, and to share their poetry and stories. But most importantly, my husband Kit—my E.B., my true north and my loving partner in life for the journey—encouraged me from the start to follow this writing road that I am now on, and that has made all of the difference in my life.

"Notes From Breakfast Creek" ended when Kit and I moved for a brief seven months in 2005 to New Mexico. Upon our return to southern Boone County, we moved a holler or two NW of Breakfast Creek to a magical five-acre parcel we call "Boomerang Creek." Once again we are down a country road, this one unpaved. It is a graceful mix of merging creeks, native woodlands and open prairie grass meadow that are home to deer, birds, squirrels, owls, turtles, frogs, moles, field mice, rabbits, raccoons and turtles. It is a world we love sharing with family, friends and our three cats—Fanny, Scribbles and Pooh—who made the journey with us from their origins in the barn at Breakfast Creek. The Missouri River is close enough for us to hear trains passing by and, once again, the constellation Orion stands guard over our pasture at night. Back home and writing again, old friends and neighbors remain constant like the seasons and cycles of life I have come to know and love here in the Heartland.

This book is primarily a compilation of some of the essays that I wrote during the first four years of my column, "Notes From Breakfast Creek." They are representative of the themes that flowed through my weekly writings—images of rural scenes, the cycle of seasons and elements, the colorful animals at Breakfast Creek, our gardens, the kitchen and food, stories of family, cities and other places traveled, and conversations in my writer's imagination. Kit appears regularly in my columns and as a result, claims to have no secrets. I thank him for his perpetually buoyant spirit, his love and for his willingness from day one to listen to each essay as it evolves from draft to finished column. He is the finest of editors and my very best friend. This book, the first of my collected "Notes From Breakfast Creek," is dedicated to E.B. who has traveled the road to writing with me every step of the way. Kit knows him well.

Boomerang Creek
Summer 2008

Acknowledgements

Many of the essays collected in this book have their origins in Boone County. I thank the countless friends I've come to know and love in Missouri where Kit and I have put down deep roots over the past twenty years. Most especially Louise Dusenbery gave me shelter the day I arrived to begin life at Breakfast Creek and took me to dig heritage irises and peonies. Orion and Barbara Beckmeyer taught me about farming, bees' wings, and canning tomatoes. With Larry "Loghead" Hall's guidance we chinked a log cabin at Breakfast Creek. Diana Hallett and I tested our talents together at Sundance. Jane Flink encouraged me to try my wings as a writer. Sally and Hugh Sprague welcomed us with boomerangs when we moved back to Missouri. The good people of Hartsburg, Ashland and Columbia leave their doors and hearts open and always have a pot of hot coffee on the back burner. The *Boone County Journal* gave my column its start early in 1994. Hank Waters and the *Columbia Daily Tribune* family welcomed me aboard in the fall of 1997. In addition, Gil Grosvenor and family at National Geographic have inspired my writing for decades. Grady Clay and Judith McCandless share my love of geography and words. Gil Porter loved "Sam" and cheers me on. Steve Weinberg gives instructive encouragement. And the Iowa Summer Writing Festival helped me think of myself as a writer.

Other stories have roots in my childhood when I traveled widely with my parents and sisters. Following each move over my father's 30-year career as an Air Force officer, mother steadfastly reassembled our home and carried on. The locations changed, but home life with my parents and three sisters—Molly, Kim and Kelly ("the girls" in my childhood) remained constant. To my mother, Alice, I give special thanks for her institutional memory of family facts and dates that keeps me on my writer's toes, and for her *Good Housekeeping* cookbook—the source of great meat loaf, macaroni and cheese, and lemon meringue pies. To my father, William E. Riggs, I give thanks for his gentle spirit, courage under fire, and for teaching me self-reliance when I ran out of gas in my pickup truck on Route WW. From Dad, I also inherited my deep appreciation of farming that started me on the road to Breakfast Creek long before I arrived.

My second family—my husband Kit, our son Hayden, our daughter Heidi, and all of the amazing Salter/Roetter clan—have made my life with Kit these past thirty years a joy. His love and support in my journey as a writer have made the completion of this book a reality. Without him, this book would not have come together.

Finally, four artists contributed the wonderful pen and ink drawings and photograph that appear in this book. Our talented daughter, Heidi (pgs. 1, 21, 39, 85, 105, 134) began writing and illustrating her own books when she was a preschooler. Wonderful Suzanne Dunaway's (pgs. 65, 127,149) zany drawings appeared in *The New Yorker* and *Gourmet* before she began baking hand made breads and went on to write and illustrate her own cookbooks, "No Need to Knead" and "Rome at Home." Margaret Halliburton (cover, pg.ii, title page) penned sketches of the house at Breakfast Creek and the log cabin and geese by the pond. Lovely Carole Patterson's photography captured my spirit. Finally, my Salon sisters remind me, "It's the mileage that counts!"

Thanks to you all.

Cathy Salter,
Boomerang Creek,
Summer 2008.

Chapter One

Images of the Rural Scene

Clotheslines

A Farm Auction

Truck Talk at Rice's Garage

Where the River Flowed

Seen from Above

Dancing in the Moonlight

Once in a Blue Moon

Clotheslines

Life is a tapestry of lines and patterns woven into a journey. On a map, lines are routes traced by the feet of past explorers. On a face, they are a lifetime of human experiences. Telephone lines and rail lines crisscross the American landscape, humming with a steady energy that can be felt and heard just as surely as a human pulse is read when a finger is pressed against a vein. Lines connect us with each other and with our past. Reading their patterns on the landscape is a journey back through a part of America's story that still has a foot in the past as well as the present. Some lines are disappearing. Cities bury cables, eliminating the need for poles and the busy network of communication and transportation wires that converged over city streets. Rail lines bypassed by history have become walking and biking trails, though the lines still remain on the land and in our memory. Though they have not disappeared, their function has changed with the times.

Clotheslines, too, are a part of America's story. They remain much as they have always been, a part of the landscape of rural America. Prairie women harnessed the winds of the Great Plains that blew relentlessly across the vast spaces that must have seemed like an ocean separating them from the distant worlds they had left behind. Each Monday, washday, sheets were transformed into sails, and the landscape was awash with white ships anchored in the backyards of rural farmhouses. A woman's domain was the home and the job of taking care of it filled most of her waking hours. At the turn of the century, there were still relatively few laborsaving devices in the American home. Women prepared food, cooked three meals a day, scrubbed the floor, raised the children, washed and hung out the laundry and did the ironing.

By the time of my mother's birth in 1919, the exhausting task of standing over a washboard and washtub was being replaced by power-driven washing machines. On farms, gasoline or kerosene engines regularly used for pumping were borrowed by the women on washdays. The time spent washing six washtubs full of clothes, an average wash load for a family of nine or ten persons, was reduced from six hours to four. Eventually, the electric storage battery or a direct electric current from a public service line running through the rural countryside enabled farm women to run their washing machine with an electric motor. Power washing, as it was called, was thought to be such an improvement over hand washing that it might single-handedly banish the chronic fatigue of the housewife, thus leaving her with surplus energy at the end of the day for the piles of ironing that followed washday.

Being a child of the mid 1940s, I have no memory of hand-powered washing machines, but I do remember my mother's clothesline. In 1955, we were living in a duplex in western Massachusetts. The two living units shared a utility room that housed a washing machine constantly in use. Winter memories of our two years in Massachusetts are of ice skating and shoveling through the deep snowdrifts that grew into mountains nearly burying our clothesline pole.

It was a modest clothesline, designed to fit into a small yard. Like an umbrella, it could be collapsed during the winter months when it was not in use. When open, its four concentric lines grew out from a single pole anchored to a cement pad. On days when the line was filled with billowing sheets, it made the neighborhood game of hide-and-seek a grand adventure.

Mother had a large wicker laundry basket and a blue-and-white striped clothespin bag that she hung on the line and pushed ahead of her as she worked her way from the inner reaches of the clothesline to its widest outer ring. I saw such a clothespin bag recently at an auction but didn't bid on it when the moment came to act. I have thought about it many times since that day, and regret that I don't have it to use on the makeshift rope clothesline strung across our basement.

While washing clothes by hand would be tiresome and tedious today, there is a quietude and peace connected with the solitary exercise of hanging up the week's laundry. It is an outdoor task, done ideally on a day when there is sun and wind moving through and around the clothes and the woman, warming them both as she stretches and bends between laundry basket and clothesline. As each item of bedding or clothing comes out of the basket, it is given a firm shake before being pinned onto the line. Patterns begin to form, and colors fall between white spaces like a quilt being pieced together. Each washday a new and unique pattern is created and taken apart in the time it takes for the clothes to dry.

Like a quilt, what hangs on the line is, literally, the fabric of our lives. Like the telephone line and rail line, it connects us to another time. It is a line that stretches between our youth and our present age. It is a place where we played in our childhood and stood next to our mothers and sisters. It is an exercise in silence. And it is a connection that I feel to all the women who have ever stood at a clothesline and let warm breezes carry their quiet thoughts and dreams up into the fresh and open air, to be carried, who knows where? (1994)

A Farm Auction

The Bax family has been a part of the history of Koeltztown, Missouri, forever. Well, at least for more than 140 years. They came when this deeply rolling foothills region of the Ozark Highlands was settled. In the period between 1830–1850, the land in Osage County was being developed in grain and livestock farms by German families like that of Herman Bax. Small, neat villages like Koeltztown, Freeburg, Argyle, Rich Fountain, and Westphalia clustered around imposing Roman Catholic churches—their sharp spires rising higher than any other feature on this Missouri ridge and valley landscape.

A week ago, a friend who has come to know some of the farmers in the Maries River region of Osage County handed me a notice of a public farm auction in Koeltztown. "It's going to be a dandy," Larry said. "A one-of-a-kind event." Herman Bax, Sr., I would later learn, had started the original farm with 300 acres, and lost his first wife in her late 20s to tuberculosis. Her sister came from Germany to take care of his four children. Herman married the sister, and they had six more children. Over the years, the farm grew and three of Herman, Sr.'s grandsons stayed on to keep the land together.

"Peter F., Ludwig H., and Leo A. ran the farm all their lives," said Larry. "Three German bachelor farmers. Only Leo is left and he'll be 90 at the end of this month. I plan to bid on Leo's old 1937 Chevy truck, and the '47 Studebaker truck is a dandy, too. This is one auction you absolutely won't want to miss. These fellows never threw anything away, and the trucks still run!"

I opened the 11" x 17" auction flier and glanced down the page. At the top, there was a brief notice from Leo A. Bax, owner of the farm. "Due to the death of my two brothers and moved into a retirement home, I will offer below listed items at Public Auction at the farm located at Koeltztown, Missouri." A brief auctioneer's note at the bottom added the only other personal details. "This farm," it said, "has been in the Bax family for approximately 140 years with this being the first auction held on the farm. Items have been well cared for and kept in sheds and 2 old farmhouses on the farm."

I glanced down the page at the kinds of items being offered for sale. Antiques. Antique Clocks and Watches. Horse Drawn Machinery and Equipment. Antique Vehicles and Tractors. Household Items. Tractor and Farm Equipment. Guns. Vehicles. Tools and Miscellaneous. What remained of the family's 140 years on the

Bax farm had been reduced by the Hurst Auctioneering Service to two single-spaced inventory columns of possessions—fragments that began to read as a family history.

The first item listed was "a handmade wall hung shrine with Blessed Virgin Mary statue in the center and a religious picture on each side, all behind glass, very ornate, over 100 years old." Most of the pictures from the old Bax farmhouse reflected the family's deep, historical ties to the Catholic Church. The most unusual was a shadow-box frame commemorating a wedding. Doll-sized figures of a bride and groom rested against a cloud-like fabric that had lost its original pristine whiteness with the passing of time. Encased in the deep frame with the figures were locks of hair cut from the bride's head and what appeared to be ancient white beans.

When the picture sold for a substantial price, I was left with questions. Were beans, easily accessible in a nineteenth century German farming community, thrown in place of rice at a Catholic wedding? Was the couple Herman, Sr. and one of his two wives, or was it the parents of Leo and his two bachelor brothers?

Leo Bax was born around the turn of the century when my maternal grandmother, Florence Bell Kasten Wheeler Shelton was born. I thought of my own ties to German immigrants. Granny's first husband, William Henry Kasten, was born to first generation, German immigrants in Schenectady, New York, about the time Leo and his brothers—third generation German-Americans—were born in Koeltztown.

My paternal grandmother, Mary Elizabeth Dague Riggs was descended from a Lutheran German immigrant, Frederick Dague, born in 1736 on the border of Germany and France, who made his way by ship at the age of 17 to Philadelphia. Within a short time, Frederick moved with his wife and two small children to Washington County, Pennsylvania, and bought his first 400 acres. Like Herman Bax, Sr., Frederick Dague soon acquired additional land nearby and his descendants remained on the land as farmers.

Three generations of German immigrants. The Dague family settling on land in pre-Revolutionary Pennsylvania, near the West Virginia border. The Bax family settling in a Missouri community of German Catholic grain and livestock farmers. The Kastens settling in urban America in the late 1800s, about the time Evangelical German farmers were making their way to Hartsburg, Missouri to farm the rich bottomlands of the Missouri River.

They came from different generations, each responding to historical catalysts that led them to different locations and life choices. Still, there are threads that connect them. Today, Hilgedicks and Beckmeyers with roots going back to the late 1800s operate family farms in the Hartsburg Bottoms. And corn from the Beckmeyer farm is sometimes sold to Elizabeth Sestak's feed store in Koeltztown.

Though miles separate them, networks exist amongst communities of German farmers. I was struck at the auction by the presence of Amish farmers who had come from Clark, a farming community three counties north of Koeltztown. For the Amish who continue to farm only with horse-drawn machinery, the Bax farm's antique equipment—kept field ready throughout the twentieth century—was made to order.

Unlike the Amish farmers, the three of us bought little that day. However, we all participated in a chapter of Koeltztown history. The farm has been bought by Gerald Groene, and the last of the old Bax family possessions have been sold. Auctions with such deep roots are rare these days. Over 2,000 people came to this auction, some from as far away as St. Louis. And though some who came were antique dealers with resale profits in mind, most came simply to take home a piece of history and to celebrate the Bax family that dedicated so many generations to farming their land in Maries Country.

After the auction, we followed Rt. P to Freeburg and turned north on Highway 63 toward home. The '37 Chevy truck Larry had coveted with a 12' grain bed, no rust, and only 63,103 actual miles had gone to a higher bidder. In its place, he bid on a Missouri Valley Creamery cup, which he got by simply leaving his hand up in the air until the rest of the bidders gave up. Diana's prize was an old green, four-speed, electric fan that she bought for $1 for her horse barn. I came home with an old 3-quart crock; with images of the day's faces and events captured on film and in my writer's eye; and with a cherry pie bought from the Country Clover 4-H Club that fed the multitudes gathered that day for the auction.

Nearly home, we slowed to turn onto the old leg of Highway 63 that runs in front of Breakfast Creek. As we did, a truck piled with antique farm equipment began to pass us on our left. It was the Amish farmers from Clark riding in a friend's truck—taking home fragments of the Bax farm that will become a part of their own family's history. Piled in the open truck bed were farm implements, cast iron seats, metal buggy frames, horse bridles and collars, wooden wheels and walking plows, and a McCormick Deering corn binder.

Waves and smiles of recognition were exchanged. Leo should be pleased, we thought. The day had been cold and gray, but it had not rained. The auction had marked an ending, but it had brought new beginnings as well. Leo Bax can rest assured that the fragments of his family's farm, now in use on an Amish farm 100 miles up the highway, will be kept field ready for generations to come. (1996)

Truck Talk at Rice's Garage

1967 was a notable year. Lyndon Johnson was in his final year in the White House, the air war in Vietnam had escalated, and the musical *Hair* was playing on Broadway. It was the year that I graduated from college and flew off to begin three years in Thailand as a Peace Corps volunteer. Locally, it was the year that Raymond Forsee of Ashland, Missouri bought a sea foam green Chevy pickup truck with 1800 miles on the odometer. Thirty years, five presidents, and a world of change later, Raymond Forsee is still driving that old green Chevy truck.

Until I saw it for the first time at Rice's Garage, that truck had probably moved through most of the past three decades unnoticed and unheralded. It was a summer checklist kind of day—one of those days when it is wise to make a list first thing in the morning so nothing critical is forgotten in the heat of the day's activity. First on my list was blackberry picking. There is no "later" when blackberries are ready to be picked. You either make time and get the ripe berries before the birds do, or they are gone by late afternoon, along with any plans for a deep-dish blackberry cobbler that evening.

The time for picking was perfect and the temperature in the early morning still pleasantly cool. An hour later, accompanied only by the sounds of ducks preening on the pond and geese grazing nearby, I had picked a gallon of sweet, fat blackberries. By then, the temperature had heated up and I was ready for my second shower of the morning.

After a second cup of coffee, I called Rice's MFA gas station in Ashland to see if they had any time that morning to do a vehicle inspection on my Chevy pickup.

"Thirty minutes be okay?" was the response.

"I'll be there," I answered, amazed at my good fortune.

A lot can happen in a thirty-minute window of time. As soon as I had the okay to come in for the inspection, I was out the door with a novel, my keys and wallet and a to-do list for the morning. Just as I got to the truck, one of the barn cats nabbed a juvenile tufted titmouse below the bird feeder. I dropped everything I was carrying on the seat of the truck and took off after the bird-nabber.

A young tufted titmouse in distress is hard to ignore. Its cry is a loud, clear, one-note whistle. At their best, they are not particularly friendly and are noisier than their lovable little cousins, the chickadee. Mr. and Mrs. Titmouse had probably taken junior out for some serious flying lessons near one of the bird feeders, a favorite hangout for the barn cats. One careless touchdown on the lawn and the cat had the bird in its mouth.

Off the cat ran to the barn with me in full chase not far behind. The parent birds sounded cries of alarm, and the young titmouse cried back loudly. A chase ensued, into the barn, out the back, around the side, and down the path that runs along the west side of the pond. Finally, the cat dashed through the brush and into the woods, stopping long enough to drop the bird ten feet away from me.

I weighed the foolishness of wading through chigger-infested underbrush against the plaintive cry of the little titmouse and made my move. I had an appointment to keep and had had enough of this drama already. Without giving the cat time to react, I charged in, grabbed the bird, felt its surprisingly powerful beak clamp down on my thumb, and decided the bird was uninjured and feisty enough to survive its near-death experience. With no thanks from the titmouse, I released it and headed for Ashland.

I needn't have worried about being late. Time, along with the overhead ceiling fan in Rice's office and waiting room, seemed to have stopped. It was 1967 again in the service bay. Raymond Forsee's faded green Chevy pickup was being worked on in the nearest service bay while Raymond talked with a local member of the Wilton Boat Club. I took the seat between the two locals.

In 1967, there had been no room in my life for a truck. It would be another three years before I was in a position to buy my first car, and when I did, it was an elm green VW bug—just the right scale to fit my life at the time. But, if I had known the world of southern Boone County then, I'd have been looking for a truck just like Raymond Forsee's green Chevy pickup.

Raymond is proud of his old truck. Paid $1800 for it second hand in 1967—a dollar, he says, for each mile on the odometer. And if he had a dollar today for each sack of grain that truck has hauled over the past 30 years, well, he'd be a rich man indeed. Unlike many features of 1967, Raymond's green pickup is a survivor, with an engine that is still strong and an owner who talks with affection about the decision he made 27 years ago to buy it.

I never did read my novel that morning at Rice's Garage. It was more interesting to listen to Raymond sing the praises of his truck and to talk about how good the berry picking had been that summer.

When my truck was ready, we shook hands and exchanged smiles. I told Raymond he should hang on to that Chevy pickup for the long haul. "It's not the age; it's the mileage that counts." And if Raymond Forsee continues to get as much mileage out of his truck as I did out of our 20 minutes of truck talk at Rice's Garage, his old green pickup is going to be hauling grain for many years to come. (1994)

Where the River Flowed

A river ran through it and became an inland sea. Brown water lived for weeks in the houses and barns that dared to risk sharing the flood plain with such a moody neighbor—the old Missouri River. The buildings are empty now, curiously out of place in the middle of this new sea. Brown. Constantly in motion. A young sea exploring new avenues far beyond the old river channel, beyond the broken levees, beyond Orion Beckmeyer's green Chevy pickup that hangs on stubbornly to the levee wall. Like the spirit of this little town, it has refused to be washed down river, out to sea. As long as it hangs on, the good folks of Hartsburg will fight this battle against more water than anyone can remember, even Henry Klemme who has lived all of his 93 years in this town.

It was a restless, wild, drunken river. A crummy guest. A reckless dancer. It took over the party. Drove out the people who lived in the houses. Emptied out the American Legion Hall where the town folks come to socialize and dance. And when the river grew tired of its fun, it flowed silently out the door, leaving behind a slippery, dark brown shadow of its outrageous dance—everywhere. It will be weeks, months perhaps, before it leaves our sight … and a lifetime before it leaves our memory.

It is an eerie thing to enter a house where the river has lived for a month. The seven-foot high brown watermarks it left on the once white clapboard walls of Hartsburg's homes and post office show how far it traveled into a town it hadn't entered since 1903. And then it was nothing like this. This time it pushed through doors and opened every cabinet in the kitchens, swam in bathtubs and closets, even moved refrigerators from the foot high cinder blocks where they had been elevated weeks earlier, setting them back where they had been, upright and filled with mud.

The river still lives all around the neighborhood where I've come to offer help. Five of us have entered an empty house and begun to deal with the river's rampage. We are up to our ankles in mud that feels and looks like thick chocolate pudding gone bad. Smells foul. Clings to everything it touches. Frogs entered the house in the owners' absence and fish swam freely in each room, exiting through the back door when the river pushed it open and caused it to warp. This river, weaving through town like a bad drunk, continues to leave its mark on all that it touches.

You wait until the river has gone and, in that dead time, anticipate the task ahead. As you wait, a dense heaviness settles into your shoulders as though you have been lifting wet mud in a grain scoop. You know the cleanup will mean days and weeks of filthy, sweaty labor. Some walls will get by only being power sprayed. Most will have to be torn out, the drywall bashed with hammers and crowbars, soggy insulation pulled out and lugged to big dumpsters. Buckled floorboards need to dry and hopefully will settle back down. If not, they will have to be ripped up and replaced, too. Kitchen cabinets, appliances, old windows, and stairwell walls—all of them have been damaged to some degree or another. The next few days will determine just how much must be done—what has to be replaced, what can be saved.

But first, the labor. The mud. You have to get it out as soon as the water level drops down lower than the door jams. Before it dries inside. People—strangers and neighbors alike—wander in to lend a hand. Those lucky enough to live on high ground feel the need to carry some of the load dumped on this little town by the river. We, the fortunate ones, are drawn to the river and the drama being played out in Hartsburg that will come to be known as the Great Flood of '93.

In our oldest jeans and highest-topped rubber boots, we attach ourselves to a house and its family for the day. Assembly lines are formed to evacuate the thick, foul mud. Shovels, long-handled squeegees, rubber gloves, buckets, Clorox, and Pine Sol are available in great quantities under the Salvation Army tent. Spirit can be found in abundance at the local fire station, now serving as the community's flood relief center. Outfitted for the attack, you become part of the volunteer crew that appears on a daily basis from nearby communities, towns across Missouri, and states as distant as Colorado, Pennsylvania, Massachusetts, Texas, New Mexico, Wisconsin, New Hampshire, and New Jersey. A map in the fire station pinpoints the network of volunteers who have reached out to touch our town.

We are at once connected by the scale of the drama. Touched by the daily scenes of the river on the TV news. Unable to stay away physically or mentally. Each wanting to help in some way. Feeling ever so grateful that we are not facing ankle-deep mud in our own homes. Maybe by being here to help, we can keep the river from somehow turning its anger on us, too. It was so huge and swollen in its anger last week that we felt compelled to come often to its edge—the seven-foot high sandbag wall in the middle of town—to be close enough to stare into the face of so much power. The sight of it is locked in the collective mind's eye and we are fearful of it still a week into its slow retreat.

We begin the time-consuming process of reclaiming this house by shoveling and heaving loads of mud. Only not for long. River mud is heavy and leaves the back muscles aching if you carry it too far, or for too long. Squeegees move mud more easily. Four or five pushers in assembly line fashion direct mud from room to room, until it finally reaches the front door. With a final shove, it flies back into the river, now almost a foot below the door jamb. It will take hours of pushing and shoving and hosing down, but finally the floor will re-emerge. The once beautiful oak hardwood floorboards were milled in Hartsburg years ago when the town had two operating lumber mills. It will be difficult to rip those up and replace them with new wood. Even now, buckled and splotchy with river residue, they have a nutty richness that seems as old as the town.

Finally, by mid-day, it begins to look like a small victory over the river has been won—in this one house at least. The mud, here just hours ago, has rejoined the river. Tired, mud-spattered and hungry, we head to lunch at the fire station café—a place to sit among new friends, share stories, and regroup energies for the labors that will continue through the afternoon and over the weeks to come. (1993)

Seen from Above

I am alone at Breakfast Creek for the next several days. Just me, the chunky old black Lab, the house, porch, and barn cat populations, and our living, breathing, exploding late summer gardens. An early routine is established on the first morning. At 5:30 a.m. the radio clicks on to National Public Radio's "Morning Edition."

There is news from San Diego of genuine excitement about Sen. Dole's choice of Jack Kemp as a running mate. President and Mrs. Clinton are vacationing at Jackson Hole, resting up for the election battles about to begin. To myself, I add a footnote to the radio news. Locally, Wayne Hilgedick, a lifelong Hartsburg farmer and solid citizen, narrowly lost his bid for Representative of the 24th District. Wayne, a quiet hero to many in southern Boone County, is known and loved as a man who never found a task "too hard" and a friend who always "works to keep the spirits of others high."

My morning routine now begins with a hot shower, while hungry house cats wait patiently at the top of the stairs. I slip on a cool cotton shift, pad downstairs in my sandals, and roust the still snoring black Lab. After feeding the house cats, opening up the house, and feeding the porch cat population, I am ready to walk down to the barn. The dog trots along while a few barn cats direct my steps to their feeding station, knowing that I might easily be distracted from the task at hand by the sight of a fresh bloom in the nearby rose garden. Finally, there are pans to be filled with cracked corn for the ducks and geese and roses to be cut for the kitchen table.

Now, it is my time. Quiet time for a cup of steamed milk with coffee, two pieces of Pepperidge Farm cinnamon raisin toast, and a slice of fresh cantaloupe. The house cats have made a dash for freedom out the library door in search of grasshoppers in the mint bed. I take my coffee out on the front deck to finish an article that I am reading in the *New Yorker*. Scooter Boots's kittens dash under and through the long folds of my cotton dress. When I finish the article, the sun has washed the yard in golden light. The distant sound of Monday morning back-to-work traffic on Highway 63 can be heard somewhere beyond the back woods. It is just barely seven o'clock.

Jane Smiley's article, "Losing the Farm: Does anybody care?" is an unsettling piece, as was her Pulitzer Prize winning novel, *A Thousand Acres*. Ms. Smiley writes unsentimentally about the present era of family farming, reminding us that "the sentimental attachment many Americans feel for the family farm may not translate into any effective means of saving it. "And," she goes on to write, "the farm bill recently signed into law will, according to some farmers, destroy most of the smaller farms that are still managing to survive."

In the *New Yorker* article, Ms. Smiley writes about a California grape farmer, Victor Davis Hanson, who in his off-farm job teaches Latin and Greek at a nearby university. In his own recently published book, *Fields Without Dreams* (Free Press), Hanson writes like a Greek of the work, pain, and frustration of his own family's passionate struggle to hang onto the Hanson farm. With the end of family farming and the disappearance of a population of real farmers, Hanson warns, America is in danger of losing its national identity. He goes on to suggest that the wrong questions ("What happened?" and "What's next?") are being asked. For the sake of farming in America, the farmer-writer suggests that the more compelling questions to ask would be "So what?" and "Who cares?"

From my comfortable porch scene at Breakfast Creek, I realize that for one, I care a great deal about the family farm. I hope very much that Mr. Hanson's Greek-inspired tale does not become the future of farming in America. I have just spent part of the last week in Hartsburg giving new life to an old house on Second Street—the first house built in the town back in 1896. Being the eternal optimist, I find myself eager to write about the spirit of that little town of farm families from the perspective that I gained while painting the lofty second story walls of that old house.

The scene from above was of white clapboard homes and neatly kept yards, front and back. Unfenced, the backyards spilled one into the next, the only punctuation being the ubiquitous clotheslines present on every family lot. Next door, Helen Wintermeyer worked in her garden while Harold Martin mended a crack in her front window; a backyard neighbor was hanging the week's wash out to dry. The sounds of children played around the edges of the backyard square created by Second St., Main St., Center St. and the alley that runs next to the old house that was my window on their world.

Looking over the rooftops, I could see the world beyond these backyards. Hartsburg's old grocery store stood out above the homes at the end of Second Street. Next to it, Dotty's Cafe maintained a steady flow of eating and social traffic throughout the morning and afternoon, and well into the evening hours. The distant sound of a train across the river was a reminder that once the Missouri Kansas Texas (MKT) railroad line ran past the business edge of Hartsburg, bringing overnight customers to the old Globe Hotel, now run as a bed and breakfast establishment by Jeanette Crawford.

At 9:00 a.m. noon, and 6:00 p.m., carillon bells from the steeple at Peace Church rang out the hour for the whole town to hear. Farm trucks raced up Nichols hill at dinnertime around 12:30 and eased back downhill an hour later on their way back to the dry fields of the Hartsburg Bottoms. There has been little if any rain recently and the cornfields will need to be irrigated unless some rain arrives soon. There is always something to be done. When I finally climb down from my ladder and finish washing the white paint from my hands and arms, it is 8:00 p.m.

An old red and white pickup pulls up and in the fading light, I recognize the driver. Orion Beckmeyer has stopped to tell me "when you see a Beckmeyer heading home for a late supper, you know it's time to quit." While Orion and his brother, Glen, have been out working on the family farm, I have spent the entire day watching the scenes of Hartsburg from above. The sounds and smells and movements of this little town make me want to live there someday and be a part of its steady, daily rhythms and seasonal flows.

Seen from above, Hartsburg remains a place where spirit and optimism live in the people who farm the local fields, come together at Dotty's Cafe, and spill over into the town's backyards. For now, it is enough to feel that, through our labors, Kit and I are about to bring new life to a century-old Hartsburg home. It is a step that makes us feel that we have a stake in the future of this small, American farming community, still very much alive 100 years after the first German settlers began farming the nearby bottom lands. Seen from above, the scene couldn't look much finer. (1996)

Dancing in the Moonlight

Full moons make people do strange things, or so the legend goes. Not just people. I saw a painting recently of bears dancing in a woods. Dozens of brown bears had gathered in a clearing to dance in the moonlight. I would like to think that animals really do dance together in those hours of darkness when the world sleeps and the woods come alive. Perhaps that is where my idea for a dance was born.

It began with an innocent conversation after Sunday dinner at Dotty's Cafe in Hartsburg. Linda and Glen Beckmeyer were talking about the three enormous concrete pads that had just been poured near the family's grain storage bins, workshop and barns on Route A. It had been a daylong family project with help from a few local farmer friends. Eight loads of concrete had been trucked in. It was a coming together of men, machines, and concrete enough to support one very impressive 35,000-bushel grain bin and two smaller ones that will stand in its shadow. Now it was time to rest.

"You know what you need to do before you put up the bins?" I said. "Have a dance. A good, old fashioned, dancing-by-the-light-of-the-moon, corn harvest celebration. It's good luck, I've heard. Especially if the moon is full."

"Is that right?" Orion asked, one eye winking.

"I have it on the best authority," I assured him. After all, I thought to myself, think of the cultures in history that would build on a site only after consulting a geomancer. These popular diviners professed that all of earth's elements must work in harmony for a building to come together in a pleasing way. Here in the Midwest, corn is almost a religion. Seas of maize yield more than one-third of the world's corn, and grain elevators stand out on the landscape like cathedrals. In the Mayan tradition, where it is believed that the human race sprang from maize, corn is used in religious rites that merge Maya and Catholic symbols. *A-maizing grain, how sweet the sound...* of golden corn pouring from combine into bins near summer's end.

From Ohio to Nebraska, from Minnesota to Missouri, Midwesterners come together late in the summer to celebrate the golden grain with roots reaching back to 5,000 B.C. At the annual Sweet Corn Festival in Urbana, Illinois, thousands will gather to watch the husking and steaming of 20,000 ears of sweet corn and to cheer on locals in the corn-eating contest. In Mitchell, South Dakota every

September, thousands of ears of colorful corn are stapled to create mosaics on the walls of the town's old Corn Palace, carrying on a century-old tradition.

The Corn Belt is a region in the American Midwest that produces eight billion bushels of corn annually—some still hand harvested by Mennonite or Amish farmers, but mostly combined by ever-larger machines. That corn will feed people on five continents, and feed America's industry and livestock as well. And still, because farmers have learned that one season of plenty is not always followed by another, 25% of the corn will be held back at year's end, to be stored in grain bins and elevators as a buffer against a bad crop the following summer.

1996 has been a golden summer in the Hartsburg Bottoms, rich again in fields of wheat, soybeans and corn. After the floods of '93 and '95, the farmers were due for a good harvest and something to celebrate for a change. By mid-September, the Beckmeyer's new grain bins will be full and the rest of their corn will be on its way to market. "A dance," I repeated to the group assembled at Dotty's Cafe, "would bring a sense of good spirit and harmony to the site of the grain bins soon to receive this summer's rich harvest."

Linda embraced the idea and quickly set the date. Thursday evening at 7 p.m. With luck, there might still be a full moon to light up the dance floor. It was to be a Beckmeyer family affair, a neighbor or two, Kit and me, and finally, my sister, Molly, and nephew, Christopher who were visiting Breakfast Creek from Katmandu, Nepal.

Glen and Linda spent the afternoon setting up a barbecue and organizing the music system and lights on two existing grain bins next to the just poured, makeshift concrete dance floor. Molly and I made a carrot cake and brought chips and salsa. Barbara and Orion supplied fresh garden tomato slices and salad. Neighbors Bob and Diane Holland brought local Missouri wines and their 18-month-old son, David. Erna and Al Beckmeyer came with another carrot cake, lawn chairs and stories of their recent 60th wedding anniversary.

It was a gathering of family and friends, generations ranging from great grand parent Beckmeyers to their red-headed great grandson, William—son of Mark and Anja, grandson of Orion and Barbara Beckmeyer, and nephew of Kathy and husband Brad Belew.

When the music started up, the celebration began in earnest. Kit and I took to the dance floor and hardly left it for the next three hours. The babies responded instinctively to the music and the cool night air. Christopher, the sole teen at the dance, let his aunt Cathy and mother Molly teach him a few steps from our own years of dancing to a juke box in 1957 when I was a shy, freckle-faced 7th grader and Pat Boone was sporting white buck shoes. I even had a dance with Linda when the men got so busy talking that they stopped listening to the music.

Country music, a few waltzes, and the soulful voice of Whitney Houston (requested for the slow dances) filled the air. It was a singularly wonderful night. That rare combination of sweet friends and extended family, good food, country music and a touch of soul, a spectacular hillside setting, a dance floor bigger than the one at the Hartsburg American Legion Hall, and a full moon the color of honey on the rise.

The air that night had a rare summer coolness about it that kept the mosquitoes away and kept us dancing late into the evening. As we danced on the brand new concrete pad and anticipated the moon's arrival, the clouds thinned and finally disappeared, revealing the night, the stars in their familiar constellations, and a regular pattern of twinkling aircraft lights passing overhead.

I wonder if the pilots that night saw our lights down below. A single, golden circle of light, surrounding our celebration of life, encircling families and generations. A gathering to celebrate the grain that will soon cover the circle with thousands of bushels of golden corn. I wonder when I will ever again dance in the moonlight on a night as magical as this? (1996)

Once in a Blue Moon

Early on the first morning of November, I found myself staring up at the ceiling fan whirling overhead on low speed. It was 3:30 a.m. and I knew sleep was gone for the remainder of the night. With that, I headed downstairs in the dark to make coffee. Outside, the moon was full and magically bright. Wrapped in an old flannel robe and with coffee in hand, I stepped into its light on the back deck and recalled the last time I looked into the face of a blue moon.

It was late June 1996. That morning, Kit and I were having breakfast when Barbara Beckmeyer called. She'd been up for hours.

"Orion couldn't sleep," she said. "He's been combining since six o'clock this morning, and probably won't be home until after ten tonight." She and her sister-in-law, Linda were cleaning and bagging soybeans that morning to be planted just as soon as each field of winter wheat was harvested. Kit offered to help bag and I offered to bring lunch over to Orion and Barbara's farmhouse.

Hours later, the four of us had just finished lunch when Orion walked in covered with a coat of fine dust. Crow's feet spread out from the edges of his suntanned face, dry from long days of moving through clouds of blowing wheat dust stirred up by the giant combine he'd been driving all morning. It was one o'clock, and his workday was not yet half over.

But no one at the table was complaining. With two floods in the past three summers, there had been little time for anyone farming in the Hartsburg bottoms to sit around with friends at all. The local farmers were clearly ready for a little relief from their battles with the river.

That evening, Kit and I drove to a fish fry at the Lion Club's park in Hartsburg. At 6:30 p.m., it was still 90° without a breath of a breeze to cool down the crowd. It was a perfect night to be outside with someone else doing the cooking. Around 8:30, the hot sun finally started its slow decline. Kit suggested that we try to find Orion out in the fields and take him a cold beer.

I headed our Chevy pickup west along Hartsburg Bottoms Road, while Kit tried to keep three full cups of beer balanced on his knees. I hadn't been to the Hartsburg Bottoms for a while and still carried images of the sand dunes left by the Missouri River's Great Flood of '93. Dunes of a depth of three to four feet had covered the very fields we were driving through. But that night, the oceans of sand were once again awash in amber waves of wheat, rising and falling on the breezes that come up just as the sun begins to set. Cornstalks that we could almost touch out each side of the truck were tall and starting to tassel.

After a long search across the bottoms trying to find the lights of the Beckmeyer combine and tractors, we ended up on the narrow road that runs atop the levee, looking at fields of wheat to our left and the Missouri River creeping in on the wetlands to our right. "Now I can officially say that I've driven my Chevy on the levee," I joked nervously, "but how in the heck am I ever going to get us turned around?" It was then that we saw the lights of Orion's combine and a beaten path leading from the levee down to our friend. I drove down the side of the levee and into a field of freshly cut wheat the color of a harvest moon. We parked and walked toward the lights flooding from the giant combine that was coming directly at us.

When the fork-filled, wheat-thrashing, wide-grinning, diesel-powered, mechanized mouth of the combine finally came to a noisy halt, wheat grain began to pour through a funnel from the innards of the combine into the bed of a two-ton grain truck. Already, two tractors were busy plowing under the wheat stubble in preparation for planting the soybeans Kit, Linda and Barbara had bagged earlier that same day.

The scene was illuminated by a blue moon—the second full moon to occur in a given month. We listened to a train passing somewhere across the Missouri River that the levee holds back from these fields. We had driven into the heart of the country and, for a few magic moments, had been witness to the seasonal wheat harvest going on all across the American Heartland.

Before leaving, Orion filled our truck bed with armfuls of fresh wheat straw for our barn. As we left our friends and Kit inched the truck by the light of the moon back onto the levee road, I thought to myself, "What a day it has been! Only once in a blue moon does it get as sweet as this." (1996)

Chapter Two
The Cycle of Seasons and Elements

Spring's Splendid Arrival

Sweet Disorder

Bees' Wings

A Taste of Autumn

Winter's Hard Edge

Winter Gatherings

Spring's Splendid Arrival

I can't not write about spring today. It is in my thoughts, in the air, in the shades of tan already emerging on the faces of farmers eager to see winter come to an end. As February wound down, thoughts of spring must still have seemed as remote to flood-weary farmers as water in a desert. Curiously, water created the desert that Hartsburg's farm fields resembled during the dry, brown months of winter in early 1994. Winds had blown useless sand deposits from the flood silts across the river bottom roads, and at times it blew us out of balance, knocking our spirits down a few notches.

But, hope springs a kernel here. Plows are again in the fields. New machinery has been brought in to spread the sand from last summer's devastating floods to depths that can be disked into productivity once again. The gaping blew hole (the term for the breaks in the levees caused by the power of eroding flood waters) at the end of Bush Landing Road is gone, remaining only as a memory of the river's final insult as it left town. And for those who drove that deserted road to cheer on the old John Deere dozer and its driver—a farmer resembling a lone Bedouin crossing a snowy desert—as the two muscled dirt into that hole for three long, cold months, there is a sense of true joy in knowing that the battle was won. The blew hole is gone. The levee has been rebuilt, reseeded, and covered with straw. The new grass will strengthen the levee's hold and some will forget that the massive washout trench ever existed. But across the river bottoms, battles still have to be waged and won before anyone farming the adjacent fields can rest easy.

The important thing is that the seeds of hope have been planted. While the winds of winter tried hard to beat us back, the winds of March have gently pushed us outside again. "For, lo, the winter is past, the rain is over and gone; the flowers appear on the earth; the time of the singing of birds is come, and the voice of the turtle is heard in our land."—Old Testament, Song of Solomon, II.

We are aware that the world around us is awakening and about to leave us dizzy with color. Like Walt Disney's 1954 Academy Award winning documentary "The Painted Desert," we wait for the artist to flick his paintbrush and spread color across the brown canvas that deserts appear to be at first glance. The floods and months of winter have taught us patience. Spring does not always come quickly, but prefers to come simply and on foot. And when she finally arrives, she brings with her the wisdom of the hills and the colors of grasses and flowers we had almost forgotten. Hints of new green, the purple of early crocuses, and the yellow laughter of daffodils.

Spring can be a tease with highs in the 50s and lows in the 30s. Sunny afternoons follow mornings chilly enough that a sweater and silk long underwear still feel like a good idea. That is the stage of spring our neighbor Louise calls "pneumonia weather." Winds 10–20 miles per hour whistle down your collar and chill the bones as you bend down to admire a cluster of butter yellow crocuses. The first official day of spring arrived Sunday with 70-degree temperatures that left our black Lab panting and our cats napping in the shade. Kit and I had our first breakfast on the porch that morning—fried eggs *al fresco* on the 20th of March. As I dressed for church, I pinned a bouquet of silk violets on my dress in spring's honor.

Warm daytime temperatures and steady March winds have dried out the gardens enough for peas and lettuce that didn't make it into the ground on Presidents' Day to be planted. Potato starts have been cut into sections, each with an eye to guide it into flower. Flowerbeds are in various stages of being raked free of the leaves and dead foliage of last fall. Busy gardeners feel healthier this week and well exercised from the bending, pulling, raking, and hauling involved in bringing their gardens back to life. Like aerobic sculptors attempting to free a statue locked within a stone, they are eager to clear away the dead outer surface so earth's hidden treasures locked in by winter can breathe again.

While the forsythia are a noisy riot of yellow along the front fences at Breakfast Creek, the pond seems unusually quiet. The hen ducks have gone into seclusion. After finding four broken duck eggs in the yard, I retrieved a few eggs before our black Lab nabbed any more of them. Two green duck eggs are now rotating in our Cackle Hatchery incubator, set at a constant 98-degree temperature. Twenty-three days to go before hatching time.

Early spring is a time for caution regarding our duck population. Female red foxes give birth to from four to nine kits (pups) in late winter or early spring. Last spring I witnessed a duck-nabbing in broad daylight while sipping my morning coffee on the front porch. A flock of grazing ducks walked blindly toward a dense cedar tree where a fox lay hiding. As the fox raced away, duck in mouth, I stood speechless, unwilling to believe the drama I had just witnessed. I came up five ducks short in a head count later that morning and am fairly certain that the fox was the culprit.

I spotted the same fox several times that spring crossing the road, running toward Louise's pasture and woods. When summer arrived, the yelping of her pups faded as they grew up and wandered off, and I grew less concerned about their diet of fresh duck. A year has passed and the red fox, or a yearling from last spring's litter, is back. I'm hoping she will feed her den of pups with juicy field mice, pond frogs, and an occasional rabbit, leaving my ducks alone to lay the green eggs I need to gather for my incubator.

Clear nights are a chorus of yelping and barking as fox and dog exchange greetings and warnings. This chorus has become one of the sounds of spring at Breakfast Creek. Each day and night is alive with sounds waiting to be heard after winter's relative quiet Take a minute to listen to the sounds of spring. Listen to the sounds of tractors plowing once again. Walk to a quiet place and let yourself be amazed at what silence sounds like in early spring. If you listen hard enough, you might catch the sounds of a country church choir practicing special music for Palm Sunday, reminding us that Easter is fast approaching. These sounds—music to our ears each Easter season—assure us that spring's splendid arrival is under way. (1994)

Sweet Disorder

Summer has hit the Heartland. July is cooking the Midwest with temperatures stuck high in the 90s. It is so hot, in fact, that this month's full moon came up hard-boiled. When thermometers from Colorado to Texas to Missouri reached past 100°, the heat buckled a stretch of Highway 63 north of Ashland. These are hot and humid, three-shower days that call for moving slowly out of doors, drinking tons of water, and running the air conditioners big time in the house and car.

Yes, these are days ripe with sweet disorder. In the yard at Breakfast Creek, damson plums that have plumped up and fallen in casual disarray lie beneath the trees that dropped them. When I am in that corner of the yard on a hot day, I pop these juicy little fruits into my mouth straight from the ground where they lie ripe and eager to be discovered. Each plum has a clear diamond of liquid sugar fixed to a seam where the fruit has begun to burst with its burden of sweetness.

Three years ago, we planted a pair of semi-dwarf peach and apricot trees near the circle of plums. Each spring since their planting, blossoms have appeared, but never developed fruit in the months that followed. Whenever the hint of late frost reached my ears, I raced outside to cover the delicate peach and apricot blossoms with old sheets or large garbage bags, turning the trees into an orchard of ghostly apparitions. Then, I waited patiently for fruit to follow blossom, as a sign that my late spring dashes in the dark had not been for naught.

This summer, ten small fuzzy peaches emerged from blossoms on the parent tree. I began to plan for a summer of cobblers, chutneys, and toppings for French vanilla ice cream, but failed to take precautionary measures against the reality of peach attrition. One by one, the sweet young gems were knocked from the tree in the night, leaving the ground below sprinkled with summer desserts that would never be.

Only three peaches remain on the tree now. Three others the size of small limes lay under the tree when I went out early this morning to water before sunrise. Each had a single raccoon-sized bite in its skin. Under July's full moon, my peaches had been spotted by a ring-eyed bandit in the night; but the fruit, still hard, had not been to his liking.

Disappointed, the cheeky coon had circled to the front of the house and climbed the porch steps. There, it attempted to abscond with a large popcorn tin filled with milk dog bones that we keep on the porch for our lazy black Lab. With deft hands, it had wrestled with the can's snug lid and finally rolled the whole container off the edge of the porch and into the bushes below, where I discovered it this morning. I have removed the raccoon's immediate temptation to a more secure interior pantry, though I know the rascal will be back, hoping to get to the last three peaches before I do.

Inside the house as well, there is an air of sweet disorder collecting here and there about the place. When summer pulls me from my desk to tend the roses and fight the never-ending battle against weeds in the vegetable garden, piles begin to form on every flat surface in the house. These are the "do later" piles—tasks to be done when time allows and stacks to be put to order when the heat finally drives me in from the yard.

Household piles multiply even faster than weeds. And it is about this time every summer that the interior gardens of our lives take on the untidy look of an ambitious garden left untended for too long. A sweet disarray of books and magazines has grown on the coffee table and end tables and bedside stands alike. Yesterday's newspaper is still unread, and a small forest of catalogues has begun to spill out of the wicker baskets where they have been collecting throughout the summer.

Like the web of an orb weaver spider, a house in summer is not quite tidy, yet not unpleasant in its asymmetry either. Patterns in the spider's web seem slightly disturbed. Each irregularity in the weaving marks an interruption in the spider's progress, the way summer disturbs patterns shaped in earlier seasons.

Inside the house at Breakfast Creek, shades are drawn in the late afternoon, adding a sense of coolness to the rooms. Ceiling fans keep air moving on hot days and only slightly cooler nights, and their whirring sounds carry me back to distant worlds. They were a part of summer visits to my grandparents' house in San Antonio throughout my childhood, and were with me years ago in Bangkok where I slept under a mosquito net with a small portable fan overhead. Like a magnet attracting metal shavings, a ceiling fan pulls you into its sweet orbit, lifting clothing loose from damp skin and tossing strands of hair into sweet disarray.

The barn at Breakfast Creek continues to be a wonderful center of benign feline chaos. Kittens meet in the air in playful, leaping combat and wrestle during the morning hours when the barn's dirt floor is cool to the touch. At noon, there is little movement in the barn except for warm air being circulated by a fan that I provide for the cat population when temperatures leave them panting. By five in the afternoon, only puddles of felines remain on the barn's dark dirt floor, as though the roof leaked cats and kittens during a rainstorm.

Summer is about being hot and slightly disheveled. It is impossible to look fresh as a daisy when you've been out in the noonday sun with the rest of the mad dogs and Englishmen. But some days, that is exactly where and when you end up in the sun. When that happens, you find yourself searching for coolness like a human divining stick, "adapting into the breathing patterns of deep water" (Michael Ondaatje, *The English Patient*).

If I am to enjoy the sweet fruits of the raspberry and blackberry patches at Breakfast Creek or blueberries from the Scrivner Farm near Wilton, there is always a degree of sweat involved, no matter how early in the morning the picking begins. Chiggers, ticks, mosquitoes, and occasionally copperheads, are out there just waiting to be disturbed. Berry bush thorns draw blood and rip even the toughest of jeans.

But all the while, you know what the rewards will be. Summer itches and scratches will be forgotten after a good shower and scrub down with Lava soap. Cool again and into your second change of clothing for the morning, all that you have endured in the berry patch will be quickly forgotten. And when your first blueberry pancake of the summer hits the griddle and breakfast begins to take shape, you are just seconds from tasting one of summer's sweetest rewards.

I don't mind that these mid-July days at Breakfast Creek have arrived full of summer heat and humidity. After all, that is the nature of summer. Life has settled into a comfortable pattern of work indoors, fruit on the vine ready for picking, and the steady rhythm of ceiling fans whirring overhead. Summer is a season of sweet disorder. I wouldn't want it any other way. (1995)

Bees' Wings

There is a swarm of activity across the Corn Belt in these early weeks of autumn. Farmers across the region are busy harvesting more than a third of the world's annual corn crop. Vigorous hybrids developed in the twentieth century by American agronomists have increased yields even while acreage planted has declined. Across the hot four-month growing season, armies of corn stalks supported by deeply dug in roots grow tall and straight, each bearing a single ear of corn—the principal food plant of the Western world.

Hartsburg, Missouri is my little window on the Corn Belt. This is farmland that breathes—its patterns a reflection of the planting seasons. Farmers who grow up on the land learn to breathe in sync with its rhythms. By autumn, soybeans planted after the June wheat harvest begin to turn golden and already thousands of acres of corn are fully-grown. Such abundance makes the land feel closed in. When the farmers sense this, crops are harvested and the land breathes again.

Earlier in the summer, I drove with Kit to the Hartsburg Bottoms and watched the Beckmeyer brothers combine wheat by the light of a blue moon. With the wheat harvest complete and soybeans planted, the brothers turned their energies to corn futures. Knowing their fields and long-range weather predictions, they invested in a shiny new galvanized corn drier and a massive cooling bin where dried grain is stored until the decision is made to sell another truckload. Under a full moon in late July, we danced on the giant circular concrete pads that are now the floors of these great bins, knowing that soon they would be filled with golden corn. As we breathed in the warm air that magical night, we could hear the land breathe out. It would soon be time for the corn harvest to begin.

The sweet corn I knew before moving to the Heartland was the corn city people recognize—a hybrid variety harvested when the meat of the kernel is in the sugar stage and the ears are wrapped in an unripened green husk. The ears of field corn are twice as big. Their hard, dented, long-toothed kernels are a rich gold, the color sweet corn achieves only after being boiled. Husks ripen, too, turning the color of ancient parchment. While this is happening, farmers wait for it to dry.

After checking the fields early in September, Orion Beckmeyer brought an ear of field corn home to show his wife, Barbara. Like the carefully planted field it had come from, its corn kernels grew in long, straight rows. I soon saw that this was not just an ordinary ear of dry corn to be hung on the door as a decoration for

Halloween. Its kernels were living fruit—over a thousand living plant embryos on this single ear of corn, each in a state of arrested development. Dried to the right moisture level by blowers in the bin and cooled for long-term storage, the kernels would maintain their nutritional food value. I was beginning to understand that harvesting corn was anything but routine work.

Several weeks later, I expressed a wish to ride in a combine. How, I thought to myself, could I hope to write about a corn harvest if I had never experienced one first hand? When the corn harvest got underway, I noticed a new activity pattern around the Beckmeyer grain bins and stopped to watch Glen, Orion's brother, check the moisture level of corn inside the new dryer bin. The bin was installed by the company that made it, but Glen was the electronic wizard responsible for figuring out the wiring that makes the computer panel talk.

Early in September, a cool, wet front settled in for the better part of a week. I turned my thoughts from combines to a series of inside tasks with fast deadlines. Our farmer friends spent their time maintaining equipment and making adjustments that would keep the harvest operation humming once the rain stopped. Each load of corn hauled up the hill to the grain bins was well-deserved payback for the crops lost in two recent flood years. ·

When a warm sun finally drove me from my desk late one afternoon, I grabbed my camera and drove down Route A toward Hartsburg. At the Beckmeyer grain bins, Glen was preparing to dump a load of corn he had just driven up from the bottoms. Mark Beckmeyer, Orion and Barbara's son, signaled for Glen to back the truck up to the auger hole. Once positioned over the hole, the entire truck bed was lifted by hydraulic pistons and a panel opened on the back gate to allow the flow of golden grain into the auger mouth. Finally, the preying mantis-like auger was activated with power from a nearby tractor, and the truckload of corn began its upward journey on a conveyor belt to the top of the massive grain bin.

While grain continued to spill forth from the truck, Glen opened the cooler bin and let me climb in. Inside was a sea of golden corn; I walked like a sinking climber unsuccessfully attempting to scale a shifting mountain of sand. I lay flat to look up at the sky through the auger hole in the grain bin's cap high above me. For a moment I imagined I was a single kernel of corn, dwarfed by the scale of the ocean I had fallen into.

Shortly after I emerged from the dryer bin, Orion and his father, Al Beckmeyer, arrived. When I learned that Orion was going down to the bottoms for a few more passes in the combine, I hopped into the family's old white grain truck and rode along. There was late afternoon sun in our faces, as the two of us shared an apple and Snickers candy bar that I had brought along. Pumpkins harvested from the Hartsburg Bottoms by the Hackman family lay in mounds in their yard as we passed by on the road out of town. Turning into the sun, we drove along a farm road lined with corn as yet unharvested until we came to the combine and a shiny green grain chariot half-filled with corn.

Of the two, it was the old red International 1460 Axial Flow rotary combine that interested me. Orion signaled for me to follow him up into the glassed-in cab. When he eased the Hydra-static lever forward, the combine began to move. Shifting a few other levers and throwing switches, the rotary blades below the cab floor began spinning. Through the massive windshield, we looked down six rows of corn stalks as high as the cab itself. Orion's task was to guide the armored, Star Wars, rocket-like, combine picker headers between the evenly spaced corn rows. As we inched along, the defenseless stalks snapped down and disappeared under the combine cab. Ears in their shucks fell onto a center-feed auger and were soon gobbled into the picker-head's throat and the cobs stripped clean. Kernels of corn were spit up into the combine's grain bin, while pieces of pink cobs and chaff spewed back out through the monstrous machine's pointed teeth.

For the final two passes, I rode on top of the combine's cab. All around me, the golden fields were washed cool by the pink and lavender hues that followed the western sun as it slipped down into the Missouri River. When we had filled the combine's bin, Orion transferred some of the corn into the green grain chariot, and filled the grain truck for its final run up the hill for the day. Our ride to the scales was in the last traces of twilight, and when Orion recorded the load's weight, I had to turn on the truck's interior light to read what he had written.

It was dark when Orion began to unload the day's final grain truck. As we stood near one of the grain bins, the moon came up full. In its light, a swarm of bees appeared to have emerged from the mounding pile of grain pouring into the auger hole. A thousand tiny pieces of pink chaff hung in the night air. "They're called bees' wings," Orion said. "One flake on each side of the corn kernel keeps it nested on the cob."

The evening ended at Barbara and Orion's farm house. From their dining room table where we shared a pizza, the three of us watched the moon continue to rise over the now full grain bins. I went home pleasantly tired, conscious of how farmers must feel at the end of a long day in the fields. Later, when I brushed my hair before going to bed, pink bee's wings flew from my hair—traces of a sweet corn harvest day that I will recall for seasons to come. (1996)

A Taste of Autumn

Oh, for the days of spoiled abandon. Those lazy summer days when the sun makes movement slow to a crawl and people think unambitious thoughts. Those days when vacations are just beginning and the possibilities for filling unstructured time seem as vast as the Pacific. Summer. That time in our childhood when we eagerly burst out of the classrooms and hallways that have held us captive for the school year, free until summer reluctantly cycles to an end.

Come September, summer begins to wear a sense of urgency on her face. Dawn comes up later. Days darken earlier. Until finally, the length of night catches daylight unaware and becomes her equal—signaling the first day of autumn. From that moment, marking marking the autumnal equinox, until the winter solstice in December, there will be increasingly less daylight in which to do all that must be done in a single day's time.

And so we grow up living the fable of the grasshopper and the ant. By late September, our internal sense of industry kicks in, telling us it is time to get cracking. Time to begin storing up provender for the long winter months ahead. Time to adjust our body clocks to the fall season and acknowledge that change comes with it, bringing a sudden coolness to the air. The reds and golds on the autumn landscape are a cautionary flag. "Don't be caught unprepared for winter like the lazy grasshopper," they seem to be telling us. "Get to work!"

At Breakfast Creek, the worker ants are busy with fall chores day in and day out. There is a modest garden of Roma tomatoes still producing plum-shaped fruit and even new flowers. The bell peppers have finally decided it is time to surrender their summer green jackets, opting for the shades of red, purple, orange, or yellow that signal they are sweet and ready for picking. Fall strawberries and peas thrive in the coolness of Indian summer days. They are summer's final treasures from the garden, sweet reminders of the time just before spring passed into summer. We savor this second sweet harvest almost more than the spring peas and strawberries; for when this crop is gone, summer will have left with it.

By late September, I have canned enough tomatoes to fill the pantry shelves, but that has not slowed the flow of tomatoes from our garden. What can one do with bowls of ripened Romas that have begun to overflow like Mt. Vesuvius in the warmth of our kitchen? If I lived in Tuscany, I would dry them outdoors for several days in the warm Italian sun. Here, I "sun-dry" them on a rack in a 200°

oven for seven or eight hours. By late afternoon, when the kitchen is bathed in the smell of warm, slowly dried tomatoes, they are ready to be stored in glass jars with olive oil, a few basil leaves, and a sprig of rosemary.

Last week I couldn't resist buying a final basket of peaches from Carol Moyer at the Red Barn, our local fresh produce market. While tomatoes are drying in the oven, the stovetop is busy with pots of late summer peaches simmering in their own sweet juices. Some will be pies to surprise our palates at the end of a late winter meal. Other peaches packed in brandy will age in the pantry for a few months before they are shared with friends.

Weathercasters have been abuzz with talk of an early freeze, and that has set everyone with a garden into a flurry of unexpected activity. Clear nights and the sudden descent of cold air from Canada have sent temperatures down to record lows, just this side of freezing. Grand Island, Nebraska, had 9" of snow—their first-ever recorded summer snow. Missouri farmers watch their soybeans nervously, knowing that another couple of weeks of sun are needed to plump the beans up before they can be harvested. May rains delayed the planting season for a whole month, so an early freeze would be an unwelcome visitor in this community of farmers.

For our backyard garden, the potential of an early freeze means covering the unpicked fruit and vegetables, and bringing pots of herbs into our sunroom where they will later winter over. The basil crop, invigorated by the recent combination of sun and cool air, needs to be cut back and pounded into a *pesto*. Unlike rosemary and thyme, basil leaves do not dry well. But they can easily be transformed into a sauce that can be stored for use in the months to come when blended with *pignoli* (pine nuts), garlic, grated *Parmigiano*, and olive oil.

Another change that came about late this summer has been our pattern of exercise. After the old slice of Highway 63 that runs past Breakfast Creek was newly blacktopped in July, it was as though the road had been transformed into our own local leg of the *tour de France*. The smoothness of the surface was too inviting to be ignored.

Each dawn, we rise to the challenge and ride between 8–12 miles before breakfast. After an exceptionally dry August, we had almost forgotten the sensation of rain. It was on one of our morning rides that we experienced the first rain in almost a month. The sun was barely up and no one was on the road yet. Neither of us made a move to head in the direction of home. For miles, we rode with our heads tilted skyward letting the fresh morning rain awaken our faces.

These mornings, we ride in air that catches the breath and blows cold down the neck and throat. We will soon have to wear another layer of clothing to hold in the body's heat until the cycling produces its own source of warmth. Gloves will be needed to keep the fingers supple enough to shift gears and grasp the handlebars. Cold rain will not be as much fun to ride in, and ultimately the elements will drive us back indoors for treadmill exercise until spring is once again in the air.

As we prepare to leave behind the summer days of spoiled abandon and enter the fall season, we will have the furnace inspected and prepare for the Hartsburg Pumpkin Festival that takes place annually in mid-October. Flannel shirts will be moved from a basement storage closet, aired on the clothesline and hung back upstairs in our bedroom closet; days will continue to be cooler and seem all too brief as they are shortened by the growing length of night. With fewer chores to keep us busy outside, there is more time for quiet reflection in the evening hours. And in the early morning hour when I lie awake, waiting for the sun to warm the dawn, there will be time to think about the coming day and the world beyond Breakfast Creek.

This morning, the radio clicked on at 5:30 a.m. The temperature outside was a record 39° for the 22nd of September. I remembered that exactly a year ago, I was in Milan at the wedding of my former student, Mark, and his Italian bride, Cinzia. For a while, I lay in the dark recalling the magic of that autumn day, now already a year past. The tastes and colors of the wedding celebration and our walk together through Venice following the wedding flooded back in the solitude of the early morning hour. A year later and a world away from that September wedding and the flavors are still very much alive in my memory.

Then, the radio captured my attention with a story of John Bowles. This expatriate writer and former Broadway composer has been living in Morocco for the past 25 years. In order to focus his creative energies solely on writing, Bowles abandoned all traces of his music when he left the country. Now, at age 85, he is back in NYC for a brief and final visit, hearing his music played for the first time in a quarter of a century. But he is not moved to stay. Writing and a quiet place have captured his heart and soul. When asked why he was returning to Morocco, the writer observed, "When you have tasted solitude once, you will from then on find a way to return to it."

There is wisdom in learning to slow down and look back. From a quiet place, it is easier to see in all directions. Solitude allows us to savor the season passing before letting it go. In moments of quiet reflection, solitude gives us back the gift of time, and prepares us for the season ahead. (1995)

Winter's Hard Edge

Thailand is a hot place in every sense of the word. Hot air, hot food, hot colors. Blindingly hot fuchsias, oranges and purples—stolen from the bougainvillea flowers that cover everything in Asia—reemerging in silks that clothe the skin with a sensation of cool lightness. In the Thai language, the word *hot* has so many nuances of meaning that it has a vocabulary of its own—hot (meaning spicy) is one word, hot (meaning temperature) is another.

In the late '60s when I was living in Thailand learning firsthand the Thai vocabulary of heat, I especially remember the iceman. Each morning, he delivered a large block of ice to the family-run noodle shop where I ate during my two-year assignment at a teacher's college on the outskirts of Bangkok. There was no refrigeration. The ice was dropped into an open hole in the floor of the shop's kitchen and covered with sawdust for insulation. As ice was needed throughout the course of the day, it was chipped from the block with an ice pick and wooden mallet and rinsed in a nearby bucket.

In that distant, Southeast Asian region of my memory, winter's edge was soft and brought only warm rain. Like the blue sapphires mined locally, ice was a gem in the rough that had to be chipped out of the ground. It was a luxury used as sparingly as salt once was before there was refrigeration to preserve food. But unlike salt, ice in hot places returns quickly to the ether, until it is captured as rain and then, as though by magic, might once again be rendered hard.

These wintry days in the Midwest, we dream of hot places as I once dreamed of Thai ice. This year, winter's hard edge has redefined cold, leaving us breathless in our attempts to describe its bite. Temperature lows have shattered records from Utah to Alabama and left Texas covered with a treacherous sheet of black ice. Embarrass, Minnesota, dropped to minus 47° below last week, only to be outdone in the record books by Tower, Minnesota, where the daytime temperature dipped down to a bone-chilling minus 60°.

As this frigid Arctic air mass descended upon the country's entire middle section, schools and highways were closed, pipes froze, cars refused to turn over, and furnaces failed to fire up. Plumbers and furnace repairmen worked overtime and weekends making house calls, and the wait for a wrecker to jump-start a car battery was more than eighteen hours in some instances. Drivers were warned to carry blankets and other emergency equipment in case of a breakdown. With wind chills dropping the already frigid temperatures down to minus 90° in parts of North Dakota, exposure to the elements for too long could indeed be life threatening.

As winter's hard edge deepened this past week, people and animals alike sought shelter and ways to deal with the big chill. Our four house cats retreated to sunny windows and curled into hibernating fur balls, only occasionally rising to stretch, turn over, and warm their other side. Our old chunky dog is now a regular fixture on her plaid pillow, dead to the world until the world is once again a warmer place.

The only evening news of interest to those held hostage in winter's hard grip is the latest weather update. We hang on the weathercaster's every chilly word and hear ourselves saying, "Amen, sister," when she reports that it was seriously cold out there today. When she points to the stalled Arctic air mass pressing down on the country's mid-section, no one speaks. As bad as the forecast sounds, we gain some comfort in learning that somewhere else in the Midwest, it was actually colder than it was in our own backyard today. Finding ourselves the more fortunate ones, we empathize and feel genuine compassion for those other poor devils, all the while thanking our lucky stars that the mercury in our local thermometers has yet to drop *that* low.

As the deep freeze settled in for a second week, our inside animals grew restless to be outdoors, and the outside animals tucked deeper into their own bodies to conserve warmth. Our geese and ducks managed to keep a small hole open on the pond as long as they stayed in the water paddling. But as soon as they left the water, ice immediately began to form. As winter's edge grew harder and worked to reclaim their only opening in the ice, a routine set in. Three or four times a day, Kit and I would bundle up from head to toe and break open the shrinking hole in the ice with a farm tool called a "mutt."

More than a week of temperatures at or below zero has made the pond not only hard, but thick. By Saturday, we were certain that the pond was solid enough to skate on. It was 10° above zero, the sun was brilliant, and there wasn't a trace of wind. By now, even I was restless to escape the house to be out in the sunlight, even if the only part of me that was exposed to the cold air was my nose. After carefully testing the thickness of the ice, we both agreed. It was a perfect morning for a skating party.

While I made a pot of chili and called a few friends, Kit ventured onto the ice. Using a snow shovel, he defined a circular lane around the pond wide enough for two people to skate arm in arm. A smaller skating area was cleared near the pond's dock. Finally, the last traces of snow were brushed from the shoveled areas with a push broom. At 11:00, the geese and ducks watched nervously from their water hole on the far side of the pond as our impromptu skating party began to collect at the dock.

While Kit and Orion played broom hockey with a rice cake puck, Barbara, Diana, and I eased onto the ice. Cautiously testing our ankles, we wondered just how long it had been since we last skated. *Decades*, said our ankles, but the ankles held us up. We were skating! And the longer we skated, the more our ankles remembered. Mine remembered being ten. All I had wanted then was to skate on winter's hard edge—on the ice that formed in our back yard that cold Massachusetts winter in 1955 when snow drifted so high it almost covered my Mother's clothesline.

Diana and I linked hands in a synchronized posture and skated around the outer lane that Kit had cleared on the ice. *Right-one-two-three, left-one-two-three, right....* Not bad, we thought. Can it really be forty years since I last skated? I asked myself. Time to sit for a minute, we all agreed. Anyone want hot coffee? Kit asked. *Boom*! Barbara is the first to hit the ice. Nothing broken, thank goodness!

The longer we skated, the more we remembered. Diana couldn't resist striking a smart pose with arms outstretched and one skate elevated behind. *Show-off!* Not to be out skated by my friend, I met Diana's challenge by skating backwards. Hey, this is easier than skating forward, I decide. Then, there is more pair skating around the two-lane course. This time, I am arm-in-arm with Barbara. Then, another *boom*! and I find myself making snow angels on the ice. Only Diana leaves the ice with a clean record. *Smartie!*

Around noon, Kit brought the camera down to capture the gaiety of the moment. Pictures were taken of each skater in some dramatic pose. We had been skating for more than an hour. Our cheeks were red with color beneath our furry caps. We were winter roses blooming against the blue-white ice. We were full of our former youth and warmed by the company of such good friends. But it was time to quit while we could still feel our toes, we agreed. Time for chili and a chance to warm our backsides next to a roaring fire.

This morning, the mercury has climbed up into the thirties. By midweek, it may even reach 60°. I hope to skate one more time before the ice goes soft and finally frees the geese and ducks from their confinement to swim where I skated just three days ago.

Moments frozen in time. Remembering the taste of ice in a hot country worlds away. Learning to skate when I was ten. This lovely moment forty years later, skating with sweet friends at Breakfast Creek. Remembering again the magic of ice—just as winter begins to lose its hard edge. (1996)

Winter Gatherings

Deep in December, the sun rises late and sets early. The burnt edges of autumn lose their fiery flair as they near the end of their spiraling fall into winter. There is sameness in the weathered bark of the logs on the cabin at Breakfast Creek, the black walnut trees, and the split-rail fences that define the Creek's edges. Even the pond has a look to it that seems more brown than green these chilly days.

At the end of the third week in December, winter claims the remainder of the year's calendar and threatens to keep us skating on her icy, mercurial moods until well into March. As winter officially begins and another calendar year draws to a close, it is a perfect time to make a list of the things we should be doing. According to an old *Farm Journal Almanac*, December is the time to:

> Sing.
> Settle up.
> Track rabbits.
> Trim the tree.
> Close the barn door.
> Find the tire chains.
> Brush snow off your coat.
> Put heat-housers on the tractor.
> Hang a wreath on the front door.
> Let the silo unloader down a notch.
> Make your own Christmas ornaments.
> Toast your toes and backside by the fireplace.
> Light a candle in someone's heart.
> Kiss your love, mistletoe or not.
> Make angels in the snow.
> Gather with friends.
> Be thankful.

After reading the list, I decided to take an afternoon walk around the pond and read animal tracks in the snow. Followed by a congregation of barn cats, I set off to read the story of the wild animals that had passed our way during the prior night.

Along the way, I recalled these words of Cotton Mather: "The source of all geographical knowledge is in the field." Directed by his words, I studied each set of tracks in an illustrated animal track field guide I had brought along. It showed me the hind feet of a rabbit moving at medium speed; deer walking; muskrat or skunk at a slow lope; mink, weasel, or ermine jumping; squirrel standing on 5-toed hind feet, and many other possible finds. But before long, the cats ran ahead of me, leaving only the story of our current walk for me to read. "We are the wind," the cats seemed to say. "Chase us to that tree up ahead and catch us if you can."

This December, an Arctic blast came through the Midwest before the official beginning of winter, freezing the surface of the pond save for one small hole kept open by the paddling of our ducks and geese. That was when I learned that cats can walk on water. From my bench at the northwest end of the pond, I waited as usual for Oatmeal, Murphy, Pearlie Mae, Willy Wag Tail, Lilly, and Bear—six of my favorite cats—to burst through the woods and tag in at the foot of the bench that has become our midway meeting place. Instead, the cats walked with fearless daring onto the ice and skated single-file out to the center of the pond.

"*Cat*-astrophe!" I moaned when my efforts to coax them back to the bank failed. In discovering the magic of ice, they had been transported in a dazzling dance to a place I could not reach. The lithe and spirited *Felis domesticus* ice capaders performed in a daring show of spinning, sliding, prancing moves as I watched in silent awe from the pond's edge.

When their ice capade came to an end, the cats proudly gathered at my feet to take their bows. "I skated on the pond once," I told them. "But it was much colder then." A long, extended freeze late one February had been an excuse for a winter gathering of friends and some spirited skating on the pond. Afterward, we'd gathered back at the house to warm our toes and toast our backsides in front of a roaring fire.

This winter, there were additional gatherings of friends at Breakfast Creek to celebrate our 14th wedding anniversary and to welcome in the season of Christmas. Then it was off to San Antonio for my niece Aliya's wedding. Deep in the heart of Texas, enchiladas, Lone Star beer, and warmer temperatures replaced our Midwestern winter fare of Honey baked ham, hot toddies, and bitter cold.

In the long months to come when winter bites with its teeth and lashes with its tail, there is wisdom in revisiting the December page in the *Farm Journal Almanac* noted above. Make time to share laughter and break bread with friends and family. Warm your spirits with dancing; light a candle in someone's heart, dream of light and warmer places. Take time to notice the world outside your window. Be thankful for the blessings of each new day and take heart. For at the end of winter, spring is never far away. (1997)

Chapter Three

The Animals at Breakfast Creek

A Tree Frog

Angels in Our Lives

Shades of Gray

Walkabout Time

Gossamer

Geese and Grass

Ella and the Great Blue Heron

Sam Walker

A Tree Frog

Writing often begins with the smallest of threads. A single word triggers a thought. A second word plays in the mind. The lines of a story begin to take shape—pieces of wool spun into longer threads that will become the weaver's fabric. This story began with the tiniest of threads—a tree frog trapped in a ball of fuzz.

Until this week, I had always assumed that the music heard on warm summer evenings at Breakfast Creek was the chorus of a multitude of contented crickets supported by an orchestra of pond bullfrogs. Invisible fiddlers and croakers reciting their notes like Pete and Repeat until they have lulled us all into a state of drowsiness. Could that be their plan? Do you suppose that once we are off to bed, they set up their music stands on the bank of the pond and play for all the ducks, geese, and fish assembled?

Our evening summer music program had to be a chorus of crickets and bullfrogs, I thought. That was before I found the tree frog in our living room. When you live with indoor/outdoor cats, you get used to finding surprises deposited here and there around the house—under beds, under foot, and especially in places where you walk in your bare feet. When summer arrives, my cats spend their time stretched out on the cool ground under shrubbery frequented by local field mice, lizards and voles. More than a few of their victims find their way into the house—sometimes dead, sometimes wishing that they were. But now ... back to that little tree frog.

This week, projects began to pile up on my desk and the dust that is a part of every well lived in house began to collect around the corners and near the most heavily trafficked doorways at Breakfast Creek. That is where the tree frog comes in.

Actually, I don't know how or where it came in. Inside the house, that is. Probably in a cat's mouth, except there wasn't a mark on the little creature. All of its tiny digits and limbs were accounted for. But, I'm getting ahead of myself just a bit. Back to the dusty corners, because that is where I found it. Hopelessly trapped in a ball of fuzz like a fly in a spider's sticky web.

At first glance, I was sure it was the dead remains of a mouse. But, I soon proved myself wrong on both counts. What I picked up was not kicking, but the softness of its body told me that it was still alive. At close inspection, it appeared to be a very tiny frog, only about an inch in length, just barely distinguishable in its fuzzy encasement. Immediately, the Florence Nightingale in me surfaced, and off I went, frog in hand, to the kitchen.

There I filled a cereal bowl with luke warm water and dipped the sad little creature in, hind feet first. Immediately the web of fuzz began to sag and legs appeared. Next the upper body. It definitely was a frog. Finally, there remained the business of pulling the layer of soggy fuzz from its skin.

I approached the mission as if the frog was a skin diver in crisis, and I had to remove his wet suit in order to revive him. I concentrated on one arm at a time, peeling back the thin layer of wet fuzz from each of the frog's shoulders, right down to its E.T.-like digits. Then there followed a pop, like the sound of fingers emerging from tight rubber gloves. The round adhesive pads on the frog's elongated digits hung on to the wet fiber like glue, letting go only after I had pulled each arm and leg to an extension greater than the tiny tree frog's body length. I was a puppeteer freeing a miniature Pinocchio, hoping that the frog would soon show signs of movement on its own.

Perhaps, in its trapped state, the frog had actually begun to hibernate in order to survive. Once freed, its color changed from gray to a vibrant leafy green with streaks of yellowish orange on its soft underbelly. As its color returned, so did its movement and spirit. "Return me to the trees," it seemed to say, "There I will sing for you all summer long." And so, I did.

Life is sometimes like the dilemma of this little tree frog. We get ourselves all wrapped up in the stuff of life and feel trapped when every minute of the day is dedicated before it arrives. The thought of so much to do leaves us almost immobilized. We dream of quiet places and envy the frog its ability to slip into a state of suspended animation. The weight becomes a great piano attached to our foot, dragging us to the bottom of the ocean.

But, like the tiny tree frog, the human spirit is resilient. At some point, we struggle out from under the weight of whatever has stolen our voice and frozen our movement. We begin to deal with one task at a time. They are manageable that way. And, if we have learned anything, we set aside time to pick wild raspberries and listen to the music of tree frogs at sundown. There is wisdom in the songs of even the tiniest of creatures. The burden is ours to listen. (1994)

Angels in Our Lives

A white cat walked gingerly across our frozen pond just moments ago. The sun's glare made it impossible to tell if the surface was water or ice. I can't imagine making that crossing, but then, I am not a cat. Cats have nine lives; mortals have just one. But what if I had had no choice. Could I have made myself as light as a feather? As lithe as a cat? Would a guardian angel have appeared at the moment of crisis to carry me safely to the other side, as weightless as its own airy apparition?

Are there, in fact, angels in our lives? During the season of Christmas, angels appear to be everywhere. We hang them on trees, bake them as cookies, recount the angel Gabriel's visit to the virgin Mary in annual Christmas pageants, and feature their cherubic images on Christmas cards and stamps. On wintry days, we create images of angels by falling into snow banks and spreading our arms and feet over newly fallen snow. Snow images of the angels we would like to be.

We are all little angels at birth, arriving into the world in a state of pure, naked innocence. As infants, we are our parents' precious angels. Then we sprout our wings, learn to stand on our own, and eventually fall a notch or two from grace during that period of growth known as the 'terrible twos.' But to some who don't have to deal with us on a day-to-day basis, our state of angelhood can last a lifetime. Aunts and grandmothers see only wings, never warts.

As a child, my grandmother, Florence Bell Kasten Wheeler Shelton, was my special angel and I was hers. Hollywood actress, Jean Harlow, had popularized white hair in the late thirties and Florence—at an age younger than I am now—had made a bold transition from the brown-haired beauty of her youth to the white-haired angel I was to know as Granny for the rest of her long life. She was present the day I came into the world, almost half a century ago, and noted that I had been born with wrinkled socks on my feet. At that same moment, I took note of her angel-white hair and sensed that no matter what happened in my life, I would never be alone.

As St. Ambrose wrote c. 380, "Angels are given to us as guardians." Some people claim to have been visited by a guardian angel; others who can't perceive of their existence profess never to have experienced them. Yet most people when asked whether or not they believe in angels answer yes. Discussions of angels have had such a resurgence in recent years that a special section has been created in some bookstores to house the array of books written on the subject.

The belief in angels has existed across many cultures over the centuries. The New Testament reminds us to "be not forgetful to entertain strangers, for thereby some have entertained angels unawares" (Hebrews XIII, 2, *c*. 65). The Koran praises the Islamic God, Allah "who maketh the angels his messengers, and giveth them two, three or four pairs of wings" (XXXV, *c*. 625). Pope Gregory the Great described nine orders of angels when he wrote, "There are, to whit, angels, archangels, virtues, powers, principalities, dominations, thrones, cherubim and seraphim," (Homilies, XXXIV, *c*. 600). And theologians during the Middle Ages pondered the question, "How many angels can dance upon the point of a pin?" (*c*. 1400).

At Breakfast Creek, angels appear in the shapes of animals and frequently arrive unannounced around Christmas time. Sam, our wonderful coonhound, appeared in the barn our first Christmas here, stayed four years, and was gone. Sam had accompanied me in my initial years at Breakfast Creek on explorations through the woods and on long walks down unfamiliar roads. He was my guardian hound and loyal canine friend—a much beloved addition to our family.

After Sam died, other animals began to appear. The first was Barney, an old yellow bruiser of a cat; then Blanche, his dainty white, adoring mate. Barney fathered four kittens and doted on them like an old daddy lion, allowing them to play with his tail and pounce on his body unmercifully. Then, following Sam's pattern, Barney disappeared. "Like angel visits, short and bright," (Norris, *Miscellanies*, 1637). Sam and Barney added much to my life in their short time at Breakfast Creek.

Our Christmas angel this year came early. He was one of three kittens from Blanche's last litter, born in our barn sometime in September. Because he weighed only a pound, I named him Pocket. While his two siblings grew fat and climbed trees like monkeys, Pocket remained tiny and moved with a kind of palsied motion. Like Dickens's Tiny Tim, Pocket's sweet innocence filled the barn with joy far beyond his weight of a single pound.

While days remained warm late into November, the sun helped Pocket keep pace with life. Though his steps were wobbly and falling seemed more natural to Pocket than walking, he gamely ran after his stronger siblings, Pug and Precious Jewel. Pocket grabbed life with a fearless spirit, totally unaware that he was moving through life with a terrible handicap.

Each morning and again before dark, I collected Pocket from the barn, tucked him inside my jacket, rubbed his little head between his ears, and brought him into the kitchen for some warm milk in hopes that his bones might grow strong and quiet his jerking motion. As I walked, Pocket rode with his paws against my chest, a pound of happy purring, observing the world through bright eyes from his warm nest inside my coat.

Early in December, Pocket rode with me in my red pickup to the Veterinary Teaching Hospital to be seen by a neurologist. For nearly two hours he was examined, observed, weighed, wormed, checked for ear mites and fever, and vaccinated. The doctors finally diagnosed Pocket's condition as probable congenital cerebellar hyperplasia. There is no treatment. He would be prone to accidents and need extra care. A guardian angel would be essential because his nine lives would be tested daily.

Over the next few days, the temperature began to drop. Then a cold early morning rain blew into the area, and I went to the barn to collect Pocket later than usual. When I entered the dark barn, I felt an emptiness that told me Pocket was gone long before I found his lifeless body in the cold grass. For the rest of the day, the feeling of emptiness hung on.

Why had Pocket come into my life and left it when he did? Did he appear because I was moving through new territory after Sam's death and was reluctant to take the step alone? Did I gain strength from witnessing his courageous spirit take hold of life? In this season of Christmas when angels seem to be everywhere, I would like to think that for a bright though brief moment, I had a very special angel in my life. The angel's name was Pocket. (1994)

Shades of Gray

It is mid-June and the sky continues to wear a weary face. Days have become a zone of shadows where there were once extremes of night and day, darkness and light, winter and spring. In the days approaching the summer solstice, the once youthful face of spring has aged and left us all feeling gray and puffy—a reflection of the sky itself.

A flock of newly released ducks has escaped under the pasture fences separating the pond at Breakfast Creek from the house and barn. I need to find the hole in the fence line later in the morning, but for now, I'm happy to let them root around in the wet grass. Only ten remain of the flock of 21 ducks that I released on the pond just a week ago. Raccoons or possums, most likely, have claimed the missing ones. Or perhaps a deadly snapper is lurking just beneath the surface of the pond.

Maybe the new flock's urge to wander is an effort to find their way back to the safe and warm brooder house where I fed and watered them for the first six weeks of their lives. In that cozy straw-filled space, life was as simple as it gets. Their youth was one continuous sunny day. A heat lamp warmed them throughout the night, giving the ducklings a false sense of security. Born in a hatchery near Lebanon, Missouri, the ducklings grew up at Breakfast Creek, untutored in the dangers that hide in the shadows of the pond world they now inhabit.

In the short matter of a single week, the survivors in the flock have experienced fear and flight. Each new enemy they have encountered since their release on the pond has taken on a face that they must learn to avoid at all costs. In matters of survival, there is no difference between night and day. Each has its enemies. To survive, the ducks must learn to move cautiously within the gray areas of the pond world, never sleeping too deeply or grazing unaware.

While it is still early and my thoughts have not gotten lost in a world of words, I slip quietly into the barn where I am a silent observer of a scene filled with innocence in its purest form. I take my seat on a bale of straw next to Lilly, the mother of three of the kittens performing acrobatic stunts in the center of the barn. Pug and Bianca, two of the other mom cats, join me at a safe distance to watch the show.

Each of their litters was delivered in a carefully hidden nest somewhere within the dark confines of the barn. My inquisitive visits were looked on as highly suspect. In league, the mother cats conspired to lead me astray each time I got too close to their precious hidden kindles.

They were, however, no match for our chunky black Lab's highly sensitive, kitten-sniffing nose. Within a short time, Sheba had located the site of each nest, and I had learned the color of each new addition to the Breakfast Creek barn cat family tree. As the kittens matured and added exploration to their initial regimen of feeding and sleep, the litters were moved, one kitten at a time, to new hiding places in or near the barn. At this stage, the mother cats began to lead their charges on daily field excursions into the maze of blackberry thickets nearby.

On several occasions, I found Lilly's three kittens huddled in a sleepy pile at the interior edge of the thicket. She had cautioned them to remain there until her return, and they had obeyed her. When I reached my hand in to stroke them, it was greeted with fierce hissing and spitting sounds that warned me to approach with caution. Lilly had taught them well, and at that moment, I was the enemy.

In the barn that morning, familiarity soon had rendered me invisible. The kittens had reached the climbing and tumbling stage of their growth, and by now had become more tolerant of my attempts to play with them. The mother cats had taken to lounging about on the dirt floor of the barn while their litters romped together in one great playgroup under their casual watch. I was simply another in the cooperative of moms watching their escapades and aerobic antics in the straw.

The barn that morning was an ideal world. A kitten colored of jet black, pure white, yellow longhair, gray-stripped shorthair, and calico. The three litters had wandered from their nests into the play area and mixed without incident. Playing together, there were no exclusionary boundaries denoting neighborhoods by breed or color. Mother cats did not caution their kittens to play only with kittens their same color. Lilly's white kittens raced up and roll down a bale of straw with Pug's calico kitten while two coal black kittens nestled into Lilly's belly as though she were their own mother. In this barn commune, the well-being and education of the summer's kitten population has become the responsibility of the adult cat population as a whole, without regard to color or lineage.

As adults, matters of territory and turf will at times reduce their feline world to black or white solutions. In time, competition for mates and food will lead to occasional cat fights in the night that leave signature scars on bloodied ears and drive the sorry loser to seek haven in another barn somewhere down the road. But for now, all is peaceful in the barn

With the exception of nuns, zebras, penguins, chocolate chip ice cream, Oreo cookies and early TV shows, few things in life are exclusively black and white. Most areas of life fall somewhere in between the two extremes. In time the animals must learn how to fend for themselves if they are to survive in the world. Still there is hope.

> "Between the idea and the reality
> Between the motion and the act
> Falls the reality." (T.S. Eliot, 1925)

After pouring cream into my black coffee, I returned once more to watch the kittens at play in our barn. I rejoice in the innocence of kittens and small children who see black and white not as opposites, but rather as complements. At peace on my bale of straw, I reflect on life's many contrasts and shades of color. There is rich promise in each new day at Breakfast Creek, where grays often give way to intense shades of color that mingle beautifully in the territory between darkness and dawn. (1996)

Walkabout Time

Spring is a time of rebirth, a riotous explosion of new life that seems to leap out of the dead of winter. Windows cry to be opened again, and the furry buds on our pear tree have swollen to the size of pistachio nuts in the warm days that late March has brought to Breakfast Creek. Signs of spring can be read in the trees and in the array of birds that have recently returned from their winter sojourns south. Signs can also be read by following the patterns of the creatures busily moving about at ground level. For me, spring is a season announced by the annual arrival of walkabout time.

Australians coined the term "walkabout" in 1578 to describe a person (or animal) who journeys or goes about on foot. These March days, something in the body clocks of the cats, dogs, ducks, geese, wild turkeys, wasps, raccoons, foxes, moles, and assorted wildly colorful birds of Breakfast Creek have made walkabouts of the lot of them. This week I was on the phone one morning with a good friend. While we shared news over a cup of coffee and the seven miles between us, morning sunlight broke across the world out our kitchen window. The conversation was cut short when I sighted a troop of mallards web-footing it down our gravel driveway, headed straight for the road. They became the first walkabouts of the spring—ducks out of water, on the loose and looking for greener pastures beyond their own.

For the duration of winter, these mallards stick close to our pond, keeping one spot on the ice open by the continuous paddling motion of their collective webbed feet. When they are occasionally frozen out of the water entirely, they simply curl up on the ice until the sun reappears and softens the pond's surface again. Then, like feathered icebreaker paddle crafts on assignment, they slip through the thin layer of ice and keep paddling for the remainder of winter's grey days. Finally, the hole widens and their world is a giant, ice-free pond again. They stretch and swim and begin to chase each other around the pond. After a great deal of splashing and wing thumping, they again notice the world beyond their pond. Eventually, they climb up the bank and rediscover the pasture and blackberry thickets where they will nest later in the spring.

I have never clipped our ducks' wings to keep the flock from leaving, and secretly panic each time they take to the air, circling the yard and house before splash landing back in the pond. I think I am afraid that they might spot a bigger pond from their lofty perspective up there and decide to fly away for good. But they don't fly away. They walk about. Not far, however. It is just part of their annual spring exploration—their getting back in touch with their world. After all, they haven't explored beyond the pond for months. On one of these pedestrian outings, a mallard hen will be followed by 3 or 4 protective drakes. While she walks without caution, they keep a watchful eye as she searches for a nesting niche that will escape the eye of our black Labs or marauding raccoons. Unfortunately, a Lab's nose can find even the most cleverly camouflaged nest.

Two years ago, Kit and I noticed that one of our mallard hens was nesting in the blackberry patch along the east side of the pond. In the late afternoon, we would sit on the cabin porch and watch as her mate swam the pond alone, waiting for her to emerge from her hidden nesting place. Each evening, she would call to him, asking if it was safe to come out. When he answered, she would fly down over the bank to him, and a reunion followed that was joyous and quite moving to witness. As the days went by, I eagerly anticipated the moment when she would troop a dozen little brown ducklings down to the water's edge. But she failed to re-emerge one evening. Three days passed before I walked up the slope to investigate and found a single piece of bone, all that remained of her.

Last year, another mallard hen created a beautiful nest on the south side of our house that blended into the shadows at the back of a small tulip bed. Over several days, she filled the nest with a dozen small green eggs and sat on them day and night, barely moving. I could watch her from a nearby bay window and again began to anticipate the moment when she would march her little family around the yard and walk them to the pond for their first swimming lesson. But it was not to be. One morning, our black Lab had several telltale eggshells on her dog pillow, cracked open and licked clean. Others were strewn around the yard. I was able to rescue three eggs and decided to relocate the nest. We placed them in a tub on a wooden deck (later dubbed the poop deck) on the pond. Unfortunately, the hen never reconnected with her nest, and I have yet to experience ducklings born in our own wilds. With raccoons in our woods and our pet black Lab that has grown fat from sucking eggs, it is a jungle out there from a duck's perspective. This spring, I am placing my hopes for hatching ducks on the egg incubator given to me recently by our friend Gil Grosvenor. And I have promised to name the first duck hatched at Breakfast Creek "Gilbert," in his honor.

But first, I need to walk about the environs of Breakfast Creek, scouting for nests carefully hidden from potential predators, even friendly sorts like me who have their hearts in the right places. Tomorrow, I will call Ducks & Ducks, Inc. in Lake City, Arkansas, and ask Dutch Noe to send three pair of mallards on the next delivery truck. Thirty-six hours later, I will get a call from the Hartsburg Post

Office to pick them up. Somewhere near our pond's edge, I will release each pair from the small cardboard box that they have journeyed in. In time, when they have become familiar with the pond, they too will become walkabouts. I will be right behind them, eager to collect the first green eggs to drop. (1994)

Gossamer

In another century, there was a time of year in England known as St. Martin's summer that described when geese are in season. Over time, language played with the word, and what was literally "goose summer" became more elegantly *gossamer*. The word in its final evolution is no longer limited in use to a single, specific season nor is it used solely to describe the creature that gave it its origins. It has become something more delicate and light, both in meaning and sound as it rolls across the tongue.

My world at Breakfast Creek has made me aware of the various meanings of the word gossamer. I have observed, for example, that a goose on land is a rather awkward looking creature and heavy of body. Yet, in water, geese glide silently with the same grace as their more elegant cousin, the swan. Airborne, geese fly in formations like the tip of a compass arrow, weightless markers pointing out the changing seasons as they fly overhead.

For four years, a large and aggressive gander named Snowball was lord and master of our north pasture and pond. He bit the hand that fed him and once almost knocked me down with his powerful body and wings when I turned my back on him. His personality never changed and his size made him fearless. Each Thanksgiving and Christmas, Kit talked of cooking Snowball's goose, but the threat was never carried out. Snowball was probably the reason so many of my ducks and geese survived each winter and spring. Predators didn't want to mess with him either.

Two winters ago, for some reason that I don't fully understand, Snowball went blind. I found him sitting alone near the pond and was surprised to find that he didn't get up when I approached. A blind goose, no matter how large, would not last long so near the woods. Perhaps the barn would be a safer place, I thought. When I was certain that he couldn't see me, I carefully picked him up, my hands just barely coming together around his soft, downy underbelly. Oddly, he put up no resistance. No attempt to beat at me with his powerful wings. Only the soft sound of a creature that knows it is defenseless.

I made Snowball comfortable on a bed of straw in one of the barn stalls, but soon realized that he wanted only to rejoin the flock. He could hear the other geese across the pond and by following their sound could find his way to them. For three days, he sat near his four friends in the pasture. Then, late in the afternoon of the third day, he followed their sound, making his way blindly across the pond to the edge of a small opening in the ice where they were swimming with the ducks. On the fourth morning, Snowball was dead.

A light, gossamer snow fell that night and froze Snowball's body onto the pond's surface. The four remaining geese sat next to him throughout the following day and occasionally nudged at his body to no avail. The next morning, Snowball was gone. We suspect that a fox dragged his body across the pond and up into a clearing in the pasture. All that we ever found was a pile of white goose down, so light that it floated into the air with only the slightest stirring of a breeze. The goose had been reduced to gossamer, airy white feathers scattered over the frozen grass. I collected the gossamer remains of Snowball and will someday use them to give the cushions of our down-filled reading chair a second life.

Though the word gossamer originally had its origins in summer, it is in the spring and autumn that I find reason to reflect on its meanings. On my walks during these seasons in and around the pastures at Breakfast Creek, I have seen what Alfred Lord Tennyson described as "all the silvery gossamers that twinkle into green and gold." To see them, you have to walk when it is still early, before the sun has warmed the morning dew on the grass.

Let your imagination go. What you see and how you define nature's gossamers will reflect the spirit that you carry with you on that walk. Gossamers may appear to you as silk caught on a dewy blade of grass, or appear to be a delicate piece of gauze discarded on the ground. I see them as tiny clotheslines scattered across a map of the American prairie, white cotton sheets of a thousand rural farmhouses drying in the wind.

In reality, the gossamers on morning grass that I now refer to are filmy cobwebs spun by small spiders. On damp mornings, gossamers can be seen billowing in the air, tethered by only the suggestion of a thread to some nearby anchor, or delicately spread over a grassy surface. I have never seen a spider floating on a gossamer sail, or a victim captured in its silken net. Only dewdrops trapped and held until the sun steals their moisture away and renders the webs invisible—turning ... *that twinkle*, as Tennyson wrote, back *into green and gold*.

Each night gossamers are rewoven and each morning recast. Like fishing nets, they are cast out just before dawn upon a sea of grass. For the writer, gossamers represent an effort to capture a moment or a person in words and, by extension touch those who read them. The writer's net captures words, gathers them in, and then recasts them. Words rewoven then become a new story. Gossamers are the parchment on which the writer leaves his or her watermark.

Goose summers. Cobwebs spun by small spiders. Words spun and cast adrift by a writer. Floating recollections of this magical place Kit and I call Breakfast Creek. (1994)

Geese and Grass

How strange that on the day following this winter's heaviest snowfall, with powdery snow covering every inch of ground in sight, and the temperature only 10º mid-morning with a wind chill of minus 5º, I find myself wondering where I can buy grass seed and what kind would be best for this region of Missouri.

Our pond is totally frozen this morning, save for a slushy circle kept open by the constant paddling of our 10 ducks. As an aside, in speaking about my ducks, I came to wonder what one calls a multitude of ducks. In the vocabulary of multitudes, there is a school of fish, a litter of pups, a flock of sheep, a pride of lions and a gaggle of geese. Most of us have heard of those multitudes. In my search, I found some of the lesser used terms for multitudes that might be of interest to some—of note, a crash of rhinoceroses, a leap of leopards, a nest of rabbits, a murmuration of starlings, an ostentation of peacocks, and … you guessed it … a paddling of ducks.

Five geese reluctantly share their pond with our ducks. On this particular morning, however, it seems to have finally gotten too cold for the geese to join the row of ducks lined up along the icy lip of an opening on the pond. The geese have trooped in a pecking-orderly line across the frozen surface and struggled in the deep snow up the east bank of the pond, right into a snowdrift.

I feed my gaggle and paddling friends each morning in the barnyard. They know the spot and the routine well, as do all of the wondrous wild songbirds that inhabit the environs of Breakfast Creek. The mix is cracked corn and scratch grain from Ashland's A & B Feed and Automotive store. A fifty-pound bag of each lasts about two weeks this time of year when grass for grazing is scarce and what's left is often buried under a covering of snow. Although I had taken some grain down to the more distant open end of the pond, the geese were intent on showing up for the morning feeding beside the barn.

I heard them calling in my direction. They had heard me, heard the clank of grain hitting the pans. Still they didn't appear. On a warmer day, they would have raced after curiosity, rounded the cedar trees, and met me at the feeding pans—sassy and nipping at my bootlaces. Ready by nature to bite the very hand that raised them from day-old goslings and feeds them each and every day. That is just the way geese are, and precisely why some people keep them as watch animals. Nothing gets past them unnoticed. One in the gaggle always remains alert—one eye open, ears trained to pick up the slightest sound, head pivoting on a periscopic neck high above a feathered body perfectly balanced on one bright orange or black webbed foot. Geese have the act of scoping out the scene down to a fine art.

By now, they should have met me at the barnyard feeding spot. But, their voices remained distant. I looked for them across the pond, but only saw a circle of ducks asleep on the ice. The ducks had become white snowdrifts with heads and feet withdrawn into their own down for warmth. Waiting out the cold. Waiting for the sun to work its magic on the ice. Waiting for spring.

There is a bed of straw in each of our barn's three horse stalls, but the stalls are too confining for the geese. And entering the barn is never even a consideration for the ducks. For ducks, the pond offers a chance for escape. One winter, I confined eight geese for three months in the largest barn stall, securing the enclosure from predators by stapling layers of heavy-duty chicken wire over the open areas around the stall walls. I transformed the barn into an aviary for large, flightless birds who would much rather have taken their chances with danger out on the pond—whether it was frozen or not. They hated it and I found myself trapped into a routine of lugging endless buckets of frozen water up to the basement of the house to thaw while the gaggle impatiently awaited my return with a fresh bucket of water for their drinking and bathing needs. And take my word, a goose deprived of its morning bath is a very distant cousin of that sweet, nurturing creature in the Mother Goose stories I was raised on.

It was a messy business, this relentless water regime. In five minutes time, the fresh water had been muddied to look just like last night's now-frozen bucket, and the area around the bucket quickly became a messy mud hole from their constant rooting in the straw and splashing as they bathed. I am wiser now about such matters and have learned that there is safety in numbers on a frozen pond. Five geese and 10 ducks seem to be able to maintain a small opening on the pond ice, even on a day that will probably not see 17 degrees at the warmest.

Curious as to why the geese had not greeted me that morning in the barnyard, I rounded the cedar trees which had hidden them from view, and found them stuck in snow drifts that reached above their plumped up breast feathers. Tired from walking across the pond and negotiating an icy slope, they must have simply run out of steam, leaned up against the banks of snow, and come to a complete halt. I could see that they needed a path cut for them, which I did. Then, positioning myself behind the gaggle, my arms spread like a giant bird, I drove them over to a spot near the barn where I had spread a fresh bed of golden straw.

Exhausted, they fell onto it without a word of protest. I had made the bed a deep one. These are large geese—the wide-bodied, domestic variety—lacking the grace in flight of their more streamlined Canada cousins. In fact, their flight rarely takes them more than a few inches off the ground.

    Their considerable weight sank them into the straw instantly, and upon impact they shifted into a nesting stance. I could almost feel warmth begin to generate where their downy undersides tucked into the soft straw. They gave off a collective sigh of comfort with their necks twisted backward and heads tucked under wing feathers until they almost completely disappeared from view. At that moment, they seemed content to wait like goose eggs incubating on a nest of straw for the sun to stir them out of their slumber.

    In the quiet that followed the flock's surrender to warmth, I withdrew across the snowy path and stepped inside the barn. This would be a fine time, I thought to myself, to sow grass seed. While the geese are sleeping. Grass sown right onto the snow, ready to ride the snowy tide down to the frozen earth below. To borrow moisture on that ride that would ready the seeds to cling to the ground's bare patches where the geese and ducks had nibbled the grass down to a wintery nothingness. Funny as it might seem, this is a perfect time to drive into town and pick up a bag of grass seed. (1994)

Ella and the Great Blue Heron

Early this morning, I came upon a great blue heron lost in dreams of soft water. We had both come to a spot along the western edge of the pond that was the last place to freeze in the night. The heron had seen two geese and a small paddling of ducks, circled around what was an opening in the ice. But sometime in the night, the mischievous old moon had reached out its icy fingers and pulled the pond's zipper tight, leaving them all to deal with the frozen elements on the coldest night they have known this winter.

It isn't easy to surprise a heron. Silent and stately in their movements, they hunt for food alone. So glacial are their movements as they wade around the edge of a pond, herons often appear to be asleep. In reality, they see all. Pencil thin and periscope sharp, they ever so slowly investigate the possibilities that move beneath the pond's surface. Fish, frogs and other small pond creatures quickly fall prey to the lightning-fast spear motion of their long pointed bills.

But last night, winter showed its mean streak and made the search for food hard. Made everything hard, most of all, the pond itself. To stay warm, the heron reduced itself by half. Facing rearward, the solitary fisher bird had periscoped its neck down into itself and tightly tucked its great head and bill into the downy warmth of its own wing. By morning, all that appeared to remain was a cold blue shadow balanced on a single stick frozen fast onto the ice.

The heron had rendered himself invisible and drifted into a deep sleep. That particularly cold night, he didn't mind being alone. Perhaps he was remembering the soft feeling of warm water against his long, spidery legs, and the silken feeling of pond muck between the digits of his shuffling, chicken-clawed feet. In that dreamy warm-water port, he floated through the hours until dawn and was still a thousand miles away when I stepped out onto the ice.

At that instant, the steel blue shadow frozen to the ice lifted upward with the drama of Arthur's Excalibur emerging from the stone that had held it captive for mythical ages. In the flash of a second, we saw each other and were both amazed. The heron, because he is rarely caught sleeping. The intruder, because I had never witnessed a heron's movements from so close a distance. For a moment, the great bird seemed to hang in the frigid air while his spindly legs unfolded and he arched his long neck downward into his shoulders. Finally, in the curious posture of heron flight, he lifted upward with the quiet power and grace of a Concorde jet, banked slightly westward, and flew off into the cold morning.

Had the heron stayed, I would have told him about Ella. Ella is one of eight geese who came to live at Breakfast Creek when they were only a few days old. Two were white Peking geese, two were gray Toulouse French geese, and two were fat white American country geese. But most exotic among the gaggle were the brown and beige African geese with their tar black bills.

As the juvenile goslings grew into adulthood, each displayed a distinctive personality and developed a signature honk. And, in the fashion of every animal that comes to live at Breakfast Creek, each earned a name that fit its manner and temperament. By the time the eight had matured from fuzzy goslings into young geese with emergent feathers and personalities, they had been given names—Poesy and Ping, Mary and Martha, Pekay and Snowball. Lastly, I named the African gander Muzi after a South African friend of mine, and his mate was named after the great Ella Fitzgerald who I once heard sing back in the early 1960s. Ella soon became my favorite.

When this winter began, only four of the original gaggle remained. The deaths of the other four geese are each a chapter in the ongoing story of the animals at Breakfast Creek. The animals here are at once a joy and a sorrow for me, because they live and move about the pastures, the woods, and the pond. In these places, out of my sight and reach, they are largely on their own. And so, the years have taught me to enjoy them each day—one day at a time.

Each winter I have lost a goose to either predators or stress related to some trauma they have experienced. Still, the remaining four continued to appear as formidable a presence as when they were a force of eight, and their naturally aggressive nature had led me to feel confident about their ability to protect themselves. I was, therefore, surprised by yesterday's events. Winter has shown me once again that it can be hard on animals living in the wild. Once again, I have been reminded that in nature, it is the fittest and quickest that survive.

Martha, the lowest slung and slowest of the four geese, had become separated from the other three. Unprotected, she was probably pursued across the frozen pond by a predator. It must have been frightened off before it was able to carry her away. For a day, unknown to me, she lay dead on the ice. By yesterday afternoon, she had become frozen to the pond's surface.

Late in the afternoon, I walked to the pond to see if I needed to widen the opening in the ice for the ducks and geese. As I always do during the winter months, I counted my flock. All of the ducks had crowded into the small-unfrozen opening that remained, but only three of the geese could be found nearby.

After testing my weight on the ice, I inched toward the opening and swung a bludgeoning tool called a 'mutt' at the hole's edges, sending the nervous cluster of geese and ducks scrambling for safety on the ice—all except for Ella, who appeared to be sleeping.

"Where's your little friend, Martha?" I asked Ella as she bobbed up and down among the ice chunks that congested the tiny opening.

Knowing that the four geese are rarely separated from each other, I suspected the worst and set out along the snowy pathway toward the north end of the pond. There I found the spot where Martha's final drama had been played out, and where I now think Ella must have witnessed her friend's death. Martha had been dead for at least a day when I found her.

I tested the ice. It was too dangerous to attempt to free the dead goose from the center of the pond. The predator, I suspected, would soon return to harvest her remains. Instead, I walked back to check once again on the rest of the flock. It was then that I saw the ice frozen onto Ella's body and realized that she was in serious trouble.

This time, I stepped out on the ice, reaching into icy water until my arm had a hold on Ella's underbelly. There was no resistance, a certain sign that she too understood the gravity of her situation. Quite possibly Ella had witnessed Martha's death and been in grave danger herself. Whatever drama took place out on the ice that day caused Ella to suffer severe stress. At that point, her body stopped producing the critical oils that make her feathers buoyant in water and maintain her body's warmth in freezing temperatures. When I found Ella, she was literally freezing to death.

A day has passed, the sun is out, but it is still bitterly cold outside. While the East Coast is digging out from under a record-breaking snow storm that has shut down air and highway transportation from Washington to Boston, Ella is sleeping on a bed of straw next to an air vent in the sunroom where my garden herbs and tulip bulbs are spending the winter. Nearby are a bucket of water and a pan of cracked corn.

When I finish writing, I may see if Ella is up to bathing in the guest room bathtub. It's not the pond, but at least the water will be warm. Then it will be time to repeat the morning routine of breaking another opening on the pond ice. I'll reassure Ping and Muzi that I am taking good care of their favorite girl. And if the blue heron is back, I will tell him to ask Ella about the place where she had an indoor warm water bath one January morning night when the pond outside was frozen up tight. (1996)

Sam Walker

This morning, the ground and sky are a white canvas of the season's first real winter snow. This is a quiet time. A time to reflect upon a Christmas gift of five years ago. I have learned in my brief time at Breakfast Creek that the animals that come into my life here are just mine on loan.

When you live in the country, the longevity of animals is less predictable than that of house pets kept inside or on a leash. Less certain because they are allowed to cross the boundaries of the pasture and wander into the back woods. Unleashed, unguarded. They are free to explore the wild places that lie at the edge of my world. I have learned that each time I open the door, there is the chance they might not come back. Cars and trucks pass down our road infrequently. Cats and dogs allowed to roam city streets have to become streetwise to survive. Their country cousins, on the other hand, cross the road fearlessly and with a casualness that can kill or maim. Sometimes does. And yet, each day I open that door, wish them a safe adventure in the great outdoors that Breakfast Creek provides for them, and feel a sense of the special gift that they are in my life when they later return.

Five Christmases ago—our first at Breakfast Creek—our daughter, Heidi, came home for the holidays. It was Heidi who found Sam. She was walking out of the barn with an armful of firewood, turned around and saw that she was being followed by a freckle nosed, black and brown on white hound that had wandered from who knows where into our barn. Heidi and I have the same kind of connection with animals, so there was never the need to talk about what should happen next. We immediately fed him, created a sheltered sleeping area on the front porch below the kitchen window, and gave him a name. He was home, and we all knew it. We never did find out where he had come from.

The young hound became "Mr. Samler", Heidi's choice of names because she was reading Saul Bellow's novel, *Mr. Samler's Planet* at the time. It was later shortened to 'Sam Walker' when we learned that Sam was not your garden-variety hound. He was, we were told, a treeing Walker hound. A coonhound. Coon hunters hunt them on cool winter nights and listen for their distinctive baying, a cry that comes from deep down in their broad chests, signaling that a raccoon has been treed somewhere deep in the woods.

Sam had a massive head, floppy black ears, muscular legs speckled with brown freckles on short white hair, and the capacity to sleep like a world class, hibernating polar bear. But two things were always certain to rouse him. The smell of food, especially cheese or chocolate. And the sound of a Federal Express or UPS truck pulling around our circular gravel drive—reawakening memories of a badly broken front leg his first year with us. Most likely he was hit by a truck while returning from a late night hunt in Louise's woods across the road. He hated trucks from then on, but never lost his passion for a coon or possum hunt under the light of a full moon.

Sam had two distinctive barks—one for trucks and one for strangers. Strangers approached the porch with great caution, never quite believing me when I said he was harmless or called him puppy. His bark and 120 lb. frame did not translate in any way, shape or form to "Puppy" for most folks meeting Sam for the first time.

His other bark came from some wild place way down in his broad chest and only came to the surface when triggered by the scent of a raccoon, possum or skunk. It was a deep, resonant, baying that filled the woods and told us that we wouldn't see Sam for the rest of the night. Those nights that he loved would be followed by 24 hours of sleep so deep that only the sound of food hitting his bowl would rouse him. His bladder seemed to go into a holding pattern. All bodily rhythms reduced their flow to the lowest rate possible. Sam had so mastered the art of relaxation that he could bark from a prone position. He was truly a character.

Local hunters often stopped their trucks to admire Sam when he and I were out on our daily walks. He was a coon hunter's coonhound. They couldn't believe how big he was. Their hounds were kept in pens, feed just enough to keep them at around 65 lbs.—hungry for the hunt. Sam, on the other hand, lived in our house, slept on a monogrammed L.L. Bean pillow, weighed 120 pounds, and lived for that occasional piece of cheddar cheese or a slice of ham that I tossed his way.

It wasn't that I overfed him. Not much really. After his accident, he was reduced to a slow walk or loping gait. After Sam's leg was broken, a vet had to put him back together with a metal plate and four screws. He was in a cast and had to be kept immobile for two months in one of the barn stalls. It was then that Sam and I developed the special bond that existed between just us. Maybe it was the occasional dish of Central Dairy vanilla ice cream mixed with milk on evenings when I felt really sorry for the guy. Sam did have the most sorrowful eyes. Ringed in black, and so mournful when he wanted sympathy. It was during that two months of inactivity that his youthful frame began to fill out. Later, when he learned to walk again on the bad leg, his body became solid, more muscular than normal, with the upper arms and chest like someone bound to a wheelchair.

That last year, however, Sam's fourth with us, he became sedentary Sam. He thinned down and his skin slipped over his eyes more and more, giving him the look of a Sharpei pup wearing a coat that was a size too large. One eye became cloudy. His movement slowed to a creaky, stiff-legged shuffle. Sleep seemed to be his only interest. Sam was aging before our eyes.

Friends told us that large dogs often develop problems with their hips and back legs prematurely. Cold weather becomes increasingly difficult for them to deal with. More and more, they come to sleep their days away and seek sunny places where they can warm their aging bones.

January 2, 1993 Sam went on his final hunt. It was a cold, but sunny afternoon. I had coaxed the cats and Sam outside for a group walk around the pond. For me, this almost daily walk was a chance to touch in with our world here. For the cats it was a grand expedition into territory they rarely explore on their own. And these walks got Sam up and into a landscape where smells triggered his memory of raccoons prowling near the pond in the hope of finding a careless duck dozing too close to the edge.

That day, Sam fell behind the group and headed on his own toward the back pasture. After circling the pond, I headed back inside with the cats. Sam usually circled back at his own speed, and either went into his doghouse or sat patiently at the kitchen window waiting to be let back in. When I checked on him a short time later and realized that he was not in his house, Kit and I searched the pastures and yard. It was Kit who finally found Sam in his old barn stall.

Sam had probably tried to get back up the four front porch steps, but his old legs just wouldn't carry him home. He may have stood there for a bit waiting to be found. That was Sam's habit. So patient, so completely laid back in his manner. Never would he bark to let us know he wanted in. Most likely, he had waited and then something must have told him he was in trouble. By luck or by plan, Sam returned to the very haven he had found four years earlier, when, as a puppy, he chanced upon the barn at Breakfast Creek and claimed an empty, straw-bedded barn stall for the night.

We found him curled up in the straw, unable to stand on his own power. It took two of us to carry him to the house, up the front steps, and inside where we set him down on his pillow. Sensing where he was, Sam pulled his legs into his body for warmth. We covered him with a wool horse blanket, and talked softly to him for a while before going upstairs to bed. I said his name a lot. Dogs know their name. Respond to the tone of voice you use when talking to them. I rubbed his big ears and cold, wet nose, and tucked the blanket around him. He seemed to know that he was home now.

Sam died peacefully in his sleep that night. But before he died, he must have stood up one final time. The next dawn we found him uncovered. The blanket was on the floor beside his pillow and he had reversed his direction. Most notably, Sam's legs were now in the posture of a strong, young hound in full chase. His eyes were closed, his face peaceful. So peaceful, in fact, that I reached to feel his body to see if he was still breathing. Old Sam had gone hunting one final time in his sleep and must have decided to keep on chasing that dream forever.

He was a Christmas gift on loan to us these past four years. Like a year, he had come and gone—a full life played out in four seasons. What a good year it was knowing you, Sam Walker. (1994)

Chapter Four

Gardens

The Purples of Spring

May Days

A Teacher's Garden

Maxine

A Perfect Sunday

Peas and Nature's Palimpsest

The Purples of Spring

I saw my first jacaranda twenty-five years ago. I had just emerged from four frigid Nebraska winters to warm my bones in the Southern California sun. It was June when I first noted these purple flowering trees, a surreal species as distant from the Midwest as I could have imagined. Tall and fernlike, the jacaranda is a Brazilian native that grows up to 50 feet in height in tropical regions of the world and can be found in some subtropical regions of America and Australia.

I would live among the jacarandas for the next thirteen years. Late each spring, I delighted anew in their show of royal color. Unlike Bradford pear trees that explode on the Missouri scene like April snow, the jacaranda's deep purple color emerges in Southern California much later. While the Midwest dances through the unpredictable temperatures of March, the sun-loving jacaranda is shedding its fernlike leaves in LA. Then, in June when midwestern pear trees are dense with green summer foliage, the jacaranda's crown is a solid mass of bluish-purple, bell-shaped flowers.

I once imagined that if I hugged the trunk of a majestic jacaranda until the end of spring, I would walk away wearing a sweeping circular skirt of purple blossoms as wide as the tree is tall. That is how their blossoms fall. Each tree casts a purple shadow of its former crown—mirroring its earlier self on the ground below. In 1903, an Australian artist from Queensland painted a couple deep in conversation under a canopy of jacaranda trees. The woman dressed in an eggshell white, turn-of-the-century dress holds a flaming red parasol over her head as blossoms cascade down like purple rain.

While jacaranda trees are not part of the world I know at Breakfast Creek, spring in the Midwest arrives with its own shades of purple that delight the heart. Purple martins return in mid-March and purple finches frequent the bird feeders. Late in the evening, spring peepers call for a mate from their bulbous throats of purplish skin, drowning out all other sounds but that of the tree frog.

The first purple of the season comes from the most delicate of flowers. Weeks before the official arrival of spring, crocuses push their way up through the cold ground. Cheered on by a few days of false spring temperatures, tiny purple crocuses surface with variegated arms outstretched and saffron tongues eager to sing spring's praises. Theirs is a joyful chorus, one that arrives with a promise that ...

> *... all that seemed as dead*
> *afresh doth live:*
> *The croaking frogs, whom*
> *nipping winter killed,*
> *Like birds now chirp and hop*
> *about the field.*
>
> (Anne Bradstreet *The Four Seasons of the Year*)

In April tiny violets blanket the grass around our old log cabin by the pond. Black raspberry canes, seemingly dead wood in winter, pulse back to life—their returning color a hint of the dark purple fruit that will mature in July. Wild plums begin blooming along woods and fencerows. And low to the ground, hyacinths thrust up their heavily scented heads and mock the more cautious lilacs that hold back their rich perfume until spring has fully arrived.

Two years ago as March was about to give way to warmth, my father died in the dawn that followed Palm Sunday. Now March is a harder month for me, and I move through it eager for signs of life and renewal that tell me I will soon be in my garden again. There I find great peace and feel my father's presence among the rows and beds I am now planning in my head.

All week there has been a cool breeze in the air, but at ground level the sun is working its magic on the land. In this window of time, Kit and I spread mulch around the base of shrubs and young trees. By evening, our arms ache from a day of hauling brush, pruning dead branches, and broadcasting well-aged manure over the tilled garden soil. In the final cool days of March, we will bolster the frame along the raised lettuce bed, and come April, assorted lettuces, spinach, and beets will begin to emerge.

From an upstairs window, I can see all that we had done over the past week. Looking through the redbud that graces the front of our house, I see swollen buds throughout its branches. Soon, wild redbuds and dogwoods will appear like delicate lace along the edges of Missouri's woodlands from Boone County down into Arkansas. Emerging from the drab canvas of winter, the world at Breakfast Creek is once again awash in the color purple. (2001)

May Days

"Do you suppose this rain will ever stop?" I asked on a Monday. "Maybe," the farmer answered with a slight pause, "but not until after Thursday." Can't plant the new packet of zinnia seeds, I thought to myself. They'd just wash away like the first batch. Don't want to put in tomato plants and peppers. The garden is so waterlogged I'd walk right out of my rubber boots the minute I set foot in it.

I can see it now. Stuck in the middle of my future Roma tomato patch. High-top rubber boots filling up with water. Sinking deeper and deeper into garden soil that has turned into muck. It would be like that old dream I used to have as a child of disappearing into quicksand. The dream went something like this. There was a cow stuck in a small pond next to a Texas live oak. The cow was sinking deeper and deeper by the minute. After struggling to get out, I would wake up in a sweat. (Was the creature stuck in the quicksand supposed to be me, Dr. Freud?) Anyway, it was the same dream every time. The tree, the quicksand, and the cow. Even fresh tomatoes aren't worth the risk of having that old childhood dream finally play itself out four decades later in the middle of our soggy vegetable garden.

I decide to forget gardening for the duration of the May rains, and fill up my outdoor time with other chores in and around Breakfast Creek. Maybe I'll check on the current kitten count in the barn. I call Sheba, our chunky black Lab, out of a deep sleep on her porch pillow, and we head for the barn. Her cold, black nose hits the straw, searching for a fresh scent. She reads the messages coming through her nasal sensors. Sniff, sniff, twitch, snort. Nothing elegant about that old girl when she's on assignment.

Sheba stops at the corner of one of the barn's three horse stalls and freezes—nose pressed into a small crack at one corner of the middle stall. I peep through an opening and see Lump, a sweet gray and white cat from last summer's crop, with four tiny kittens. Meanwhile, Sheba's nose moves to an old, ratty quilt hanging between two sawhorses that are supporting an inverted desk in temporary storage. The quilt is almost hidden under the bulk of the old desk.

I peek inside. Pug, a black and white cat I had mistaken for a male until that moment, was inside the suspended quilt with three fuzzy black kittens and one calico. Smaller than my fist, they already know how to hiss and spit with convincing ferocity at anything that appears threatening. Still, I couldn't resist reaching my hand in to pet them when Pug left the hanging nest to eat.

One more hiding place is soon discovered in a grain bin in the last barn stall—two white kittens, one with a black spot on its head. Suspecting that Lilly and Scooter Boots have already moved their litters from the busy scene in the barn, Sheba and I head for the woods to find them. But this is really just an excuse to take a walk in the light rain in our woods.

Last week when I took my pickup in for its 30,000-mile maintenance check, I set myself up in the waiting room at the dealership while the truck was being serviced. I had some editing work to do, and I was alone. Lovely, I thought. No TV. No one smoking. Just the soft hum of distant conversation in the hallway. The first hour flew by without an interruption.

Then the morel man appeared out in the hallway with a story he was burning to tell. For the next hour, it was like the movie "Groundhog Day." The morel story was repeated again and again, like my recurring quicksand dream. The same tree where the mushrooms were found. The same detailed recounting of the size, color and count of the man's morel harvest. I could see the scene as though I had been in the woods watching from behind the next ash tree. In fact, after the mushroom man left and another customer finally joined me in the waiting room, I found myself telling him the morel man's story, not leaving out a single detail. The morel story had become my own.

That afternoon, the sun momentarily came back out at Breakfast Creek. After days of rain, it was as though a light had been turned on outdoors, banishing the gray cast over us. Setting the wet grass a-twinkling. Glistening like a field of diamonds in the light.

Within minutes, steam rose from the ground as the earth warmed to the sun's therapeutic touch. Suddenly, I remembered the morels. Conditions were perfect. Heat following rain. Little spongy fungi were probably pushing their pointed heads up through the forest's leaf-covered floor at that very moment. In France, farmers use large-snouted pigs to hunt for highly prized black truffles. Maybe, at the northern edge of the *Aux Arc* (French for Ozarks), I might have the same luck with our wet-nosed, kitten-sniffing, low-slung black Lab.

In spring, following a rain shower, the woods at the edge of Breakfast Creek is a magical world all its own. Brown leaves of winter cushion every footstep like a soft moccasin. Between two trees, an impression in the wet leaves outlines the spot where three deer stopped for awhile to sleep. Then a flower. Wild Sweet Williams. A mass of sensitive wood ferns and white Trillium. A sea of common blue violets.

So tiny and delicate was the forest garden growing up through the brown leaves that I forgot my search for morels. Instead, I found myself imagining Alice in this wooded wonderland, running for cover as giant raindrops cascaded through the forest canopy. What green umbrella would she run under to stay dry? The answer lay at my feet. A colony of May Apples (*Podophyllum peltatum*) stood tall with their edged, parasol-shaped leaves shading the ground below their long, slender stalks.

Under the umbrella leaf of the May apple, a single white flower appears that is reminiscent of an apple blossom. Late in the summer, you can smell the apple that emerges. Maybe it was the fruit of this plant of many names—Mandrake, Raccoon Berry, Wild Lemon, Hog Apple, May Apple—that Lewis Carroll's Alice ate just before she grew tall. Perhaps, like me, Alice had grown tired of searching for morels and took pleasure instead in simply walking amongst lacy ferns and delicate spring flowers, like the silent deer that glide by unnoticed just within the forest's edge.

In May, beauty for some is in the impassioned annual hunt for the much-prized morel mushroom. For me it is the solitude of a walk through a bed of May Apples and the hint of summer when fruit will emerge from spring blossoms and warmth is again in the air. (1996)

A Teacher's Garden

My life as a teacher has made me a patient gardener. The union of my occupation and avocation happened quietly and gradually, until they had become one and the same. I realize now that my strength as a teacher related powerfully to the quiet times that I spent tending and learning from my garden.

For a good part of March and April this year, my garden took care of itself. Once the peas and lettuce had been planted and poles erected to support the young pea plants, I busied myself tending to the work that had begun to pile up on my desk. Then it rained, the yard had its first mow, and a business trip took me away from Breakfast Creek for a week. I returned to find that Kit had given the yard and pastures a second mow, a new pile had grown on my desk, and my gardens that had exploded from their quiet beginnings screamed for attention. Less than an hour after unpacking, I was reclaiming the front iris beds from an encroaching onslaught of Crown vetch, a clover-like creeping native plant that was threatening to swallow the entire garden. By early evening, I could feel myself slipping into the comfortable rhythm of gardening that I had put aside earlier in May.

The following morning, I turned my attention to the herb garden. This small 17' x 20' fenced garden is home to my Winterthur English shrub roses, two dwarf blueberry bushes, strawberry plants, and my perennial herb collection—mint, chives, rosemary, oregano, sage, bee balm, elephant garlic and assorted varieties of thyme. Last winter, I wrapped the rose and blueberry shrubs in thick bricks of straw bound together with twine and spread the remaining straw over the herbs and strawberries. After the last threat of frost, the straw was pushed aside. Two life-like black scare cats with green marble eyes were attached to the fence to keep birds at bay as the strawberries returned to life. However, in my absence, this small, controlled space had become wild and chaotic and threatened to disappear beneath a long rooted, invasive weed resembling celery leaves. As I opened the swinging gate to the garden, the perennial herbs and strawberry plants were no longer visible It was only a matter of time before the roses and blueberry shrubs would be swallowed up as well in a sea of native weeds.

Entering the garden that morning, I literally put time aside. The soil and plants were wet from a gentle drizzle that had begun in the night and continued for the remainder of the morning. Free of the constraints of a wristwatch that might pull me back to my desk, it was a perfect time to weed the garden, I was free to let my thoughts wander in and out of the boundaries of the garden, sometimes taking me to unexpected places. As I searched out last year's strawberry plants and herbs, my thoughts revisited former classrooms. The slow and exacting task put me back in touch with each individual plant in the garden, and I was reminded of the patience that it takes to be a good teacher.

Each fall, the familiar names and faces of last year's students are replaced with new names and individual personalities that must be learned and nurtured during the course of the new school year. On that first day of school, each class is a sea of unknown faces in the teacher's garden—green plants, one indistinguishable from the next. Knowing and caring about them as individuals seems a daunting, exhausting, almost impossible task. For some, teaching and gardening are chores done but rarely enjoyed. An impatient teacher, like a half-hearted gardener, allows the garden to get out of control and ultimately loses interest in gardening altogether. A constant gardener, on the other hand, like a good teacher, works patiently to achieve a balance in their garden that allows the beauty of each individual flower to stand out amongst a riot of color.

I have known many wonderful teachers over the years—some my own teachers, some colleagues from the years when I was a classroom teacher myself, and still others teachers I have taught. Mr. Arthur W. Day, my tenth grade world history teacher, had a plain face and wore narrow ties with white long-sleeved shirts and argyle socks with loafers. But his classroom was filled with the color and passion of all that had happened since the world began. History was his passion; and through his stories recounted as a living picture of peoples and cultures across time, it became mine as well. Over the years, I was inspired by English teachers with literary names like Mead, Mather, Freick, and Dowell and fell in love with a geographer who taught me how to see and explore the world. What they all had, these selfless teachers who gave so much of themselves to their students, was passion and enormous patience. They loved what they taught, and shared with students a passion for learning and exploration that challenged them to grab life. With patience and energy, they guided their students while giving them space and air to grow on their own.

Sunday afternoon, two friends offered to teach me the art of fly-fishing. When they called, I had a million other things that needed to be done, but I chose to go fishing—to sit for three hours in a canoe, focused on making the spider fly on the end of my line find its way to a particular spot on the surface of the water. They were good teachers, sensing when to instruct and when to leave me on my own. I don't remember exactly when it happened, but at some point in the afternoon, the rhythm of fly-fishing became natural. At that moment, I stopped thinking about what I was supposed to do and allowed the act of fly-fishing to instruct me. These friends, my teachers that afternoon, are farmers. The sense of balance that they find in a life of farming and their passion for fly-fishing is not unlike the balance in my life as a teacher and gardener.

For much of my teaching career, I have followed my hours in the classroom with hours in my garden. There are lessons in the time spent in the quiet tasks of a gardener that I am certain have made me a better teacher. Perhaps, if I had discovered fly-fishing earlier, the same lessons might have been learned while standing in a cold mountain stream. There are lessons to be learned from both. The art is in having the patience to be still long enough to hear the words. (1994)

Maxine

In October, Paris is the color of light. Trees in shades of gold and the oranges of autumn's fiery sunsets line the boulevards along the Seine. Fragments of the city's history and art reveal themselves around each corner, washed in warm colors that leave me close to tears. Together they are a prism through which I now reflect upon the day that I first met Maxine.

It was difficult to leave Paris that week, even for part of a day. But it was my birthday, and I wanted to see Giverny—the world painted by French Impressionist artist Claude Monet at the turn of the 20th century. That morning, after a stop at a neighborhood *boulangerie* to buy *pain chocolat* to eat with our morning *café au lait*, Kit and I walked to the *Gare Saint-Lazarre* station and caught the train to Vernun.

Monet painted this Paris train station scene in 1877 filled with blue clouds of vapor billowing from an arriving steam locomotive. The artist and his second wife, Alice, chose to live in the countryside where they were only an hour by train from the art world of Paris. Claude and Alice loved food trips to Paris that provided them with delicious opportunities to bring new recipes back to their cook, Marguerite, from favorite restaurants in the city.

An hour after leaving Paris, our train pulled into the small station at Vernun in a light autumn drizzle. Our 6 km. walk to Giverny took us through scenes painted by American Impressionist artists who were drawn to Monet's village early in the twentieth century, as well as landscapes painted by Monet himself. Past turn-of-the-century French country houses with small gardens, narrow cornfields along the Seine, and bold flowers that mirrored the colors of autumn. Finally, a sign—*Musee Claude Monet*, 1 km.

We walked the length of *Rue Claude Monet*, passing stonewalls and two-story houses ablaze with fiery red ivy. The temptation was to wander up one of the side streets and find a house to rent. Then stay 10 years to paint the scenes visible from the hills that Giverny looks out upon. That was when we saw a house painted in colors unmistakably taken from Monet's own palate—a rectangular two-story pink stucco with white trim and bright green shutters.

From the moment we stepped from the narrow cobblestone lane and entered Monet's studio adjacent to the family house, I felt my heart racing. Massive canvases of Monet's pastel water lilies hung around the open room and a life-size, sepia-tone photograph of the artist himself stood in an open doorway. Through the doors of the studio, we entered *les jardins de C. Monet*. (Monet's garden) While Kit sat on a green bench to capture our walk from Vernun in his journal, I headed off on my own, disappearing down the parallel rows of flowers that spilled out from the front of the house, still not believing that I was really there.

The garden world that Monet created in his studio was exactly the world that I was walking through. His famous purple irises had died back after their spring bloom, followed in summer blooms of yellow and orange nasturtiums that spread in unruly masses onto the gravel pathways. Beds of still blooming roses were interspersed with raging fuchsia and pink colored cosmos. The *jardin d'eau* (water garden) was the same pond that I had seen many times in his paintings, though in the fall, his oft-painted water lilies were dormant. His distinctive green Japanese bridge, the green rowboat, the graceful weeping willows and stunning sugar maples were all unmistakably part of his signature and design.

On that late October afternoon, I walked alone in Monet's gardens until I came to the stone passageway that connects the flower gardens to the other side of the pond. There I passed a tall woman wearing a peaceful expression that mirrored my own. We had each been transformed by the beauty of the artist's gardens. As we floated past one another, neither of us found it necessary to speak.

Several hours later, the woman—Maxine Martell—rode with us on the train back to Paris. She and I talked with excitement, both of us exhilarated by the day and the realization that the three of us had been in Monet's world virtually alone. For an afternoon, we had each walked the pathways around his pond and rested on the wooden benches Monet provided for moments of quiet reflection. The artist had left them there for us, we imagined. In my mind, I saw Monet at work. His brush was a maple tree, dipped in red and splashed across the glass surface of the pond. In the green boat, elegant young ladies in long white dresses and straw hats rowed effortlessly through the floating lilies, emerging from the scene as fresh as when they stepped into the scene a century ago.

Back in Paris, that same memorable day, Maxine joined Kit, our son Hayden, and me at Les Bourgeoises—a tiny restaurant near the Place des Vosges—for a Parisian dinner *extraordinaire*. Later I wrote the following in my journal—

> *A new friend made the day even more wonderful. Maxine found us in Monet's gardens and we all seemed to sense that the conversation should continue. She is an artist seeing France and Italy for the first time. Somehow we hope to know her for years to come, for it seems we have known her from time past.*

It has been three years since that magical day at Giverny and our dinner with Maxine in Paris. Each October, she sends white tulip bulbs for the gardens at

Breakfast Creek. Kit and I had only visited Maxine through letters until last week when travel took us to Seattle. After a day of exploring the Pike Street Market and sampling the bookstores and coffee shops that line Seattle's old downtown, we took a ferry to Whidbey Island and the world that Maxine and her writer/husband, Jim, have created.

The afternoon and evening were filled with conversation that recalled our day together in Giverny and our mutual excitement at seeing Monet's world in the same light that he was a master at capturing—first outdoors, and later in his studio. Then the conversation turned to Maxine's art.

Maxine and Jim built their house, Maxine's studio and a small guest cottage in an open field and filled each with color-both inside and out. In this open setting, light washes over each small unobstructed structure Light also comes from these two themselves and the works that they create from within their sanctuary.

Each room is alive with eclectic objects from their pasts. Everything is immediate, useful, and rich in color and texture, catching light from a sky that changes throughout the day. It is this light that gets them up finally from their separate studios. Pulls them out to the nearby beach or down the quiet road where they walk their Scottish terriers, Butter and Nell.

I now have Maxine's world in my mind's eye. I see her at work in her pink studio trimmed in white, in her garden of red poppies and white roses, in her kitchen that smells of apple tarts and fresh coffee, and sitting late in the evening with Jim as they listen to a Canadian Public Radio broadcast of one of Michael Ondaatje's novels—imagining scenes in the dark as the author paints stories with a brush of words.

In the middle of the night, I walked alone from the guest cottage where Kit and I were sleeping to Maxine's studio, guided by the narrow beam from a flashlight. A stuffed Felix the Cat toy and a Raggedy Ann doll sat motionless, guarding the studio in the darkness with open-eyed expressions. A bowl of dried poppy pods and a plate of three red pears joined other objects that would take on another life, along with the seated woman who shows up again and again in Maxine's art.

I entered the studio in my bare feet, not making a sound, but the woman in Maxine's canvases was awake and saw me come in. "Night," she seemed to say, "is when the woman puts down her mask and walks freely about the room." In the dark, I saw her step out of one canvas in a lime green dress and dance in a pair of red high-heeled shoes. When I entered the studio the following morning, the woman had returned to her seated posture, masked again from the light that reveals too much.

Maxine is now working in her studio on Whidbey Island, and I am at Breakfast Creek in mine. We seem only to meet in time frames that barely span a day.

Nonetheless, each new October when I see the world awash in autumn light, I think of Paris and a woman named Maxine who, like me, was transported by the color and light that live on in Monet's garden. (1995)

A Perfect Sunday

The beauty of leaving New York early on a Sunday morning is watching the city awaken. Manhattan's streets are never without people or taxis. It is simply that there are fewer of them at 5:30 a.m. on a Sunday. Joggers run silently past shrouded forms of urban homeless. Taxis lurk near hotels hoping for a lucrative dawn airport fare.

Around town, *New York Times* addicts are already afoot, eager to buy a Sunday paper at the nearest corner market. They pass lean joggers wearing "Just Do It!" running gear and feel at peace with their own decision to read rather than run each Sunday morning. Years of experience have taught them that carrying a hefty issue of the Sunday *Times* for more than a block passes as physical exercise. For the city's literati, a perfect Sunday begins with a pot of coffee, a Danish, and the *Times*—quite literally, a forest of knowledge and the source of countless conversation topics for the week ahead.

After a week of exploring New York City on foot and by subway, I felt in synch with its rhythms but out of touch with the world of southern Boone County. The prior month had been one of steady deadlines and travel that kept me away from my vegetable garden and distant from friends in Hartsburg. For much of July, I had been unable to enjoy the antics of this summer's crop of Breakfast Creek barn kittens or the progress of crops planted late in the Hartsburg Bottoms because of May flooding.

A week after my return, I awoke just before dawn with no particular plan in mind for my Sunday. In the country, 5 a.m. hardly ever seems early. Since it is the coolest time of the day, the thought of sleeping in is simply out of the question. By the time Kit has our morning coffee perking, the barn cats have their bibs on and the geese are pacing their pasture, impatiently awaiting the sound of cracked corn hitting their metal feeding pans.

This Sunday after the dawn barn detail had been completed, I cut a handful of fresh roses and walked up to the house. Following my nose, I entered the kitchen through the pantry door. Kit was frying bacon and had four large country eggs ready to crack onto a hot griddle. Slices of Pepperidge Farm white toasting bread were in the toaster. Orange juice and apricot jam were already on the counter. While the eggs were frying, I steamed a small pitcher of milk for our coffee and carried the *Columbia Tribune* out to the breakfast table on the screened porch.

That is how my perfect Sunday began. There was time for an easy breakfast, a coffee refill, and a start on reading the Sunday paper. Then it was time to dress for church. That morning, Kit was scheduled to teach a special Sunday school class on the geography of the Holy Land. We noted that the Mays and the Underwoods had come an hour earlier than they normally do to participate in Kit's talk, and enjoyed the exchange of ideas offered during the lesson.

Following the service, we caught up on news with friends for almost an hour. I congratulated our emeritus pastor, Herschel Hughes, for losing 14 pounds through disciplined calorie counting, and learned that Erna and Al Beckmeyer had recently celebrated 59 years of marriage. The community welcomed us back into their comfortable circle as though no time had passed at all. No questions asked. No explanations to be made about our absence the prior Sunday.

As we were about to leave, an invitation came to share a noon meal of sweet corn, green beans, and tomatoes with Orion and Barbara Beckmeyer. It was a meal in which everyone participated in getting the food from the garden to the table. The men picked corn and visited in the shade of a tree while they husked each ear. The women cut beans and sliced tomatoes. It was a fresh-from-the-garden feast that rivaled the finest meal Kit and I had eaten while in New York. The extraordinarily sweet tomatoes tasted as if they had been sprinkled with sugar, and not a person at the table could imagine the need for dessert.

It was early afternoon before we arrived back home. The animals by then had retreated to the cool underworld of low-lying shrubs to sleep away the heat of the mid-afternoon sun. Following their example, Kit stretched out for a short nap, but I knew that I wouldn't be able to rest until I had restored some semblance of order to the garden. It was an essential step that I needed to take that Sunday to get back in touch with the rhythms of Breakfast Creek. For the next hour and a half, our two Russian Blue cats, Kashmir and Jammu, kept me company while I weeded. Characteristically, not once did either cat lift a paw to help.

Around 4:00 p.m. I was in the blackberry patch down by the pond. It was in this very berry patch just over a year ago that I reflected on the benefits of pruning to explorations in various urban neighborhoods in New York City. Now once again, I was back, trying to get in touch with my own world at Breakfast Creek. By the time my bucket was full of blackberries, my thoughts had traveled to Paul, an old friend in Los Angeles who recently shared with me news of his cancer, and to a longtime friend, David, in Santa Fe who hopes to run a marathon when he turns 50 in a week. I had also thought of my youngest sister, Kelly, teaching in Guatemala, and my older sister, Molly, who lives with her family in Nepal.

Finally, my thoughts returned to our local friends who had shared their garden provender with us that noon. What would make this a perfect Sunday, I thought, would be returning the favor, with one addition. I called Orion and Barbara and invited them to come over with their fishing poles. There would be a chicken roasting in the oven, I told them, in case the fish weren't biting. After fly-fishing on the pond, we could enjoy the corn and tomatoes they'd sent home with us earlier in the day, along with the rest of the meal.

But this time, there would also be dessert. There was a bucket of freshly picked wild blackberries to be shared and a carton of Central Dairy vanilla ice cream in the freezer. All we needed was for our two friends to help us sample those berries. That is how my perfect Sunday played itself out. Short on fish. Long on friendship. Sweet from beginning to end. (1994)

Peas and Nature's Palimpsest

A palimpsest is a tablet, twice written on. A sheet of parchment, written on, erased, and written on again, until only traces of earlier markings are legible. In the city, streets are that tablet. Seen from underground, layers of each road reveal the passage of historical time in the same way that a limestone bluff records geologic time at work on the land. In nature, earthen layers are laid down, erased, uplifted, worn down, and built up again. In cities, there are layers of concrete, Macadam, brick, cobblestone, gravel and sand. Near the bottom, dirt paths trace the course of human movement through the early city, laid down over animal trails from a more distant past.

In nature, time and the seasons are the palimpsest. By late February, winter has erased most traces of the summer past, leaving the world at Breakfast Creek a weathered wooden gray. The cedar additions to the limestone house, the century-old white oak logs of the cabin by our pond, and the barn's old wooden doors age comfortably with the passing seasons. In winter's final stages, when few traces of green can be found on the land, their weathered textures melt into the world around them.

As I stood on the porch Sunday afternoon, I saw someone walking toward the driveway with a small boy. When they turned into the driveway, I realized that it was Mrs. Quinn and her great grandson, Ricky. I noted with interest that they were some distance from her house down Lloyd Hudson Road. The unseasonably warm 70-degree temperatures that had pulled me outside had taken Mrs. Quinn farther than she had intended on their walk. When I offered to drive them back, she owned as how she wouldn't mind. But first, if I didn't mind, Ricky would like to visit the kittens in the barn. "Of course," I said.

I was glad to drive my neighbor home. When Sam, our old coon hound was still living, I walked several miles down Lloyd Hudson Road three or four times a week, often stopping to talk with Mr. and Mrs. Quinn about their gardens and raspberry vines. When Kit and I took up cycling on our freshly blacktopped road last summer, the Quinn's gravel road no longer suited our exercise circuit. While the cycling has introduced me to new neighbors at the distant end of our slice of old Highway 63, I have missed my walks down that old gravel road.

When I drove Mrs. Quinn and Ricky home, I looked over at their recently plowed garden plot between the driveway and fence line. Each spring, the Quinn's two daughters and sons-in-law put in a garden shared by the three families that produces a rich harvest of vegetables from early spring until the first serious frost. Eight years ago, when I planted my first ambitious vegetable garden at Breakfast Creek, it was their garden that was my guide for when to till, what to plant, and when to harvest.

"Has Barbara planted peas yet," I asked?

"She's already got them in," Mrs. Quinn answered, pointing to the nearby garden plot.

"Me, too," I announced, proud that my garden was keeping step with the Quinn's.

Garden fever of the late February type had already grabbed more than a few of us this past week. In the eyes of this gardener, there is nothing quite like peas in simplicity and their delicate beauty. By week's end, unseasonably warm days had made the garden's soil pliable, and rumor has it that Anna and Walter Sanderson had already gotten their peas in.

Clearly, it was time to get peas into the ground before winter decided to march back onto the scene. Earlier in the week, I had stopped by Strawberry Hills nursery to see if Joyce and Gary Sapp had sugar snap and snow peas for sale yet. A closed sign was posted on the barn door. Nonetheless, bless her kind heart, Joyce produced a pound of the very peas I was hoping to find.

A garden is part of nature's palimpsest. Erased in the fall. Ready to be written on as each new spring approaches. Early Friday morning, I approached the blank page that was last summer's vegetable garden, prepared to write "peas" on the lines where traces of last year's vines were just barely legible in the dirt. Accompanied by our four house cats and our chunky old black Lab, I wheeled a barrow filled with freshly dug compost into the garden and began digging two-inch trenches on either side of the sturdy wire fences that supported last year's pea vines.

While the cats raced from one end to the other in one of the fresh trenches, I spread compost and scattered dried peas along the others, covering them with a final layer of compost and garden soil. Our cats love this garden more than any other place at Breakfast Creek. While I garden, they dig and roll and attack each other in the soft, sun-warmed dirt. Later in summer when the garden has been written on more completely, the leafy rows of crops offer a haven of cool, green shade.

Now that my peas are in, it is time for patience. For legume-loving gardeners deep in the winter blahs, the wait for spring's first pea crop can seem impossibly long. It will be 65 days before the earliest peas appear on the vines. During the waiting period while we dream in Technicolor pea green, we should give thanks to

Clarence Birdseye who turned peas into one of the first frozen vegetables back in the 1920s. Frozen peas were his greatest success story.

Peas frozen right after they are picked stay remarkably green and tolerably fresh tasting. Blanched in boiling water for 3–4 minutes, the bright peas appear to have popped out of their freshly picked pods just moments ago. Some of the earthiness and sweetness of fresh peas is lost in the freezing process, but cooked *al dente* and tossed with butter, a few sprigs of fresh mint, and a dash of salt and pepper, they are still a treat. Without a doubt, one of the sweetest marriages ever made in American culinary history has to be hot buttered peas and homemade mashed potatoes served with meatloaf on a cold winter night. In the depths of winter, Birdseye comes to our rescue with those little bursts of brilliant green that lift our spirits and leave us ever hopeful that spring will return before too long.

Early this morning on National Public Radio, I listened to an interview with a wildlife biologist who has studied a pack of Rocky Mountain wolves in Glacier Park for the past 17 years. Diane Void explained that she does not try to find the wild creatures for fear of disturbing their natural patterns. Rather, she reads the wolves' traces before they are erased from nature's palimpsest. Their scat patterns. Their scent marks. The remains of their kills. She has also learned to return their calls in the wild.

"People say I am so lucky," the wildlife biologist remarked in the interview, "but they are wrong." She went on to say that she had made choices. Given up having children. Given up the comforts of home. Now 17 years later, she has chronicled better than anyone ever has the patterns of glacial wolves in the wild. This, she reminded us, did not happen without significant personal sacrifices.

Cozy in our warm bed, I thought about the choices Diane Void has made in her 17-year effort to read the faint traces left by glacial wolves on nature's palimpsest. But, I noted, she forgot to mention peas. Her choices have forced her to give up gardening and the chance to ever plant a crop of fresh spring peas. At that moment, 65 days no longer seemed like such a long time to wait. (1996)

Chapter Five

Food and the Kitchen

Sweet Apple Times

Hand Made Breads

Corn and Tomatoes

Comforting Thoughts

American Pie

Garam Masala

Sweet Apple Times

It is early on a late September morning. Though the sun has risen, the sky is as dark as night. I am sitting with my morning coffee on the front porch, witnessing the first rainstorm of autumn. The electricity in the atmosphere has pulled me outdoors to be a spectator to nature's rumbling bowling tournament taking place overhead. Madame Butterfly, Morgan, and Willy Wag Tail—three kittens from this summer's crop of barn cats—are chasing dry leaves across the covered porch and playing with the laces on my walking shoes. I am reluctant to turn on my computer to begin writing down the story taking shape in my head.

The black walnut trees drink in the rain and drop their green fruit onto the lawn that has had its final mow of the season. Their nut lies locked within a thick green husk coated with oily black tar. Over the summer, the green spheres have grown as big as crabapples, and to tell the truth, I wish that they were. They would be my orchard, and Breakfast Creek a world of apple trees.

In my imaginary orchard, an apple tree up slope from the barn is an aged York Imperial, planted a century ago by John "Appleseed" Chapman. As my friendship with the tree grows, I watch the gnarled old tree for signs of the passing seasons and learn about the animals and birds that this venerable tree watches over for me.

Late in April, a male robin can be seen perched on a nest in the apple tree. In the morning sun, he watches for the return of Mrs. Robin who has been out collecting breakfast for their eternally hungry offspring. In early May, I lean against my tree's sturdy trunk and catch the clear light filtering through her outstretched branches and apple green leaves. When I spot the first pink and white blossom emerge from a cluster of velvet green, I know that the apple tree and I have survived winter's final bite.

In July, long after the sweet smelling blossoms have made their transition from flower to fruit, the old tree patiently feeds the young apples while another summer season is recorded on her trunk. With a rat-a-tee-tap-tap-tap, a yellow-bellied sapsucker probes for sap and insects, drilling holes that have left the tree pock marked all around and up the face of its weathered trunk. Sticking out of its bark, the sheath of a barn cat's claw is all that remains of a drama played out under the tree's graceful canopy.

By late August, the round-faced Yorks in my imaginary apple orchard have grown red and freckled. They are like children baked a rosy brown in the sunshine of late summer—reluctant to give up their freedom when summer ends. They have seen caterpillars lunching on the tree's leafy greens and watched moths emerge from gauzelike tents hanging between branches. When apples fall, some are eagerly rolled into holes dug by squirrels that now bound across the great mother tree's branches. Others that roll under dry, autumn leaves will remain hidden until deer root them out in winter's first snow late in November.

The rain has stopped now and, to my great disappointment, the fallen apples are once again clearly walnuts. Still my flight of fantasy has reminded me of sweet apple times in my own past. Twenty years ago, Kit and I spent a delicious day with our children, Hayden and Heidi, in Oak Glen—a California orchard community known as "Appleland" nested in the San Bernardino Mountains east of Los Angeles. Memories of that day together and of baskets filled with Red and Golden Delicious, Rome Beauty, and tart Pippin apples still hang crisply in my mind.

In the town of Hartsburg, not far from Breakfast Creek, apple butter time arrives just before the autumnal equinox. On a Friday evening, 30–40 town folks gather at the American Legion Hall to begin preparations for making apple butter—a tradition local families have maintained for the past 100 years. Over the course of an evening, 30 bushels of Jonathan apples trucked up from Farris Orchard near Camdenton, MO, are prepared for cooking the following morning. Peelers are positioned on stools at the four corners of a large table filled with aluminum tubs. For three hours, four manual Klean Kutter apple-peeling machines are kept in non-stop motion by a cast of volunteer peelers that changes whenever someone's cranking arm needs a rest.

Apples impaled on the Kutter's spike have their red jackets unzipped with a few fast cranks of the machine's handle. Perfectly peeled, they are tossed into a nearby tub and delivered to a wide circle of men, women, and youths seated in front of washtubs lined with sheets. Just as fast as the peeled apples are delivered, the hands of the seated volunteers work with paring knives over bowls resting in their laps, filling the tubs with cored and sliced apples. At evening's end, the whirring noise of the peeling machines and the chorus of chatter and story swapping of the peelers is quieted. The 28 bushels of apple slices are covered for the night with the sheets they are nested in. Back home, the peelers soak their fingers, stained black from apple acid, in lemon juice or Clorox before turning in for the night.

By 6:00 a.m. the following morning, four wood fires are burning behind Hartsburg's American Legion Hall. It is 40° outside and the men tending the fire are dressed in layers of flannel and bibbed overalls. In the kitchen, women check each apple slice for bruises and imperfections. When the coals are hot, a large copper kettle is nested over each fire. The kettles, burnt black on the outside by a century of apple butter making, are polished copper bright on the inside. To each kettle, Lauretta Hilgedick and her legion of apple butter worker bees will add two buckets of water, 70–80 pounds of sugar, and 3 ounces of cinnamon. Around 6:30 a.m. they begin adding sliced apples a batch at a time, until each of the four kettles has received its full measure of apples sometime around 10 that morning.

From 6:30 a.m. until 2:00 in the afternoon, the kettles are constantly stirred to keep the butter from burning. Men take turns stirring the bubbling, cinnamon brown apple butter with handmade wooden paddles attached at a 90º angle to long handles 5–6 feet tall. Each rectangular paddle has had large flow holes cut into it to keep the apple butter moving evenly. Like the copper kettles, these old paddles have remained in the same families now for generations.

When the apple butter has thickened, Lauretta—reigning Queen of the Worker Bees—emerges from the kitchen with a green saucer onto which she spoons a dab of hot butter from each kettle. A kettle is deemed done when the water has cooked down enough for the butter to hold firm when the saucer is inverted. At that time, the hot apple butter is ladled from the kettles directly into sterilized quart jars. Back in the kitchen, women in assembly-line fashion wipe the jar rims clean, apply a lid and firmly screw on a ring to seal the lid.

By afternoon's end, almost 600 quarts of apple butter have been filled. An hour or so later, the pinging sound of the jars sealing can be heard around the room—sweet music to the ears of all who have labored to fill apple butter orders for the community. Outside, Carl Thomas is busy cleaning each of the paddles and copper kettles, readying them for two more apple butter sessions scheduled for later the same week. The count at week's end is 1630 quarts.

Come autumn in Hartsburg, making apple butter is a community affair. Hilgedicks, Sandersons, Brunes, Lengers, Thomases, Hackmans, Barners, Bockhorsts, Begemanns, Zumwalts, Georges, Guiers, Reifstecks, Glascocks, Klemmes, Keenes, Nichols, Brashears, Barnetts, Bueshers, Cunninghams, Longs, Crammers, Walkers, Wilsons, Salters, and other families take part in this century-old, German heritage tradition. Throughout the winter months, these sweet apple times will be revisited each time a quart of apple butter is opened in a Hartsburg kitchen.

As this rainy Monday morning moves toward afternoon, I cut an apple into round slices, each with a star in the center that was once the core. The poet Robert Frost liked to slice apples that way. No waste at all. Were he here, I would describe the world of my imaginary apple orchard, and recount how apple butter is made in Hartsburg. For Frost, apple time was a sweet time, indeed. One filled with edible stars, each at the center of its own divine constellation. (1996)

Hand Made Breads

Bread, it has been said, is the staff of life. It is the substance around which many of the world's people build their daily diet. It is so basic, so nutritious, and yet, so simple in its body of ingredients. The bread of history's ovens is a combination of three basic ingredients—flour, salt, and water. But like so many simple things in life, there is an art to how the three are combined. That art is the story of great breads.

There is a geography to baking bread. Egyptians mixed grain meal with water and made flat bread by baking their dough on heated rocks. Greeks learned bread making from the Egyptians and taught the method to the Romans. By the Middle Ages, bakeries could be found in most European cities. Today, the art of bread making has become the passion of a new generation of home bakers. That is where my story begins.

Fifteen years ago, Kit and I bought a French baker's table. This very solid, handcrafted table supposedly dates back to the French Revolution. Its surface, scarred by use and time, is etched with the stories of the thousands of loaves of bread that it has given rise to over the past two centuries. When I run my hands over the character marks etched into the old table's worn surface, I can almost feel the floured hands of the French bakers at work shaping bread for the revolution's hungry masses.

Three years ago, we visited our son, Hayden, in Paris. Each morning began with a trip to the corner *boulangerie* for a baguette of bread and a few *pain chocolat* to dip in our morning coffee. Bakeries appeared to be a fixture in every neighborhood of Paris that we walked through, and bread became a central part of our every meal. We returned to Breakfast Creek with a hunger for crusty loaves of French bread and a neighborhood bakery of our own.

A trip to Milan two years later reintroduced me to Italian *pane* and the wonders of *foccacia* made with olive oil and rosemary or black olives. I had first tasted *foccacia* bread in the kitchen of Don and Suzanne Dunaway, good friends and neighbors from our days living up Beverly Glen Canyon in Los Angeles. Suzanne, a gifted cook, began making a few loaves of *foccacia* bread each morning before breakfast and soon found a demand for her special breads at a local restaurant and market. A year ago, she opened her own bakery, *Buona Forchetta,* where she and Don now bake hand made breads daily for some of the finest markets and restaurants in the city.

I came away from Suzanne's kitchen after a recent visit to L.A. with a loaf of her bakery *foccacia* in my luggage. With it came the smell of rosemary and images of Suzanne holding a basket filled with loaves of her hand made breads baked that morning in the industrial-sized convection ovens she and Don have installed in their Italian *moderne* kitchen. To keep the memory and flavor of Suzanne's bread alive, I've planted rosemary in my herb garden at Breakfast Creek and keep a pot of rosemary in a kitchen window so it will be on hand when I don my own baker's apron.

Time is the fourth, unwritten ingredient in bread making. No matter how you slice it, making bread from scratch takes time. When our daughter Heidi came for a visit recently, we talked about bread machines. She is a vegetarian and loves breads made with stone-ground organic flours. Though she prefers to make bread by hand, the time involved has moved her to consider buying a bread machine.

Knowing that Heidi's birthday was coming, I researched articles in food and cooking magazines ranking bread machines currently on the market. Williams-Sonoma advertises a bread machine they like so much they have given their company's name to it. *Cook's Illustrated* tested ten bread machines and ranked the National Bread Bakery machine as having "the best shaped loaves with great crust" and the Zojirushi Home Bakery machine as "the machine with the most powerful computer chip."

Ultimately, I shared my findings with Heidi but left the final decision on bread machines up to her. Soon afterwards, I took my friend, Jane Flink, to lunch at *Trattoria Strada Nova*, a superb Italian restaurant in Columbia. Dining at *Trattoria* always begins with a basket of Tuscan bread and a saucer filled with olive oil. Bread is at the heart of the Italian dining experience, and so it is natural that bread worked its way into our conversation.

After sampling a plate of hot biscuits and apple butter sent by Chef Michael Odette to our table, I asked Jane what she thought about bread machines. "Make your own bread," she responded without hesitation. "It takes time, but the bread always tastes better." Following our lunch, I bought Martha Rose Shulman's book, *Great Breads: Home-Baked Favorites from Europe, the British Isles & North America*. I decided to put aside the idea of purchasing a bread machine until I had read what the author had to say about bread making and had tested a few of her recipes.

In her introduction, the author attributes her fascination with bread to living in Paris for 12 years, just half a block from the city's most famous bakery—the Poilane bakery on the rue du Cherche-Midi. There, she would take friends to watch the baker, "wearing only boxer shorts and sandals, work one of three eight hour shifts, mixing up the dough in a huge mixer, shaping 40 five-pound loaves and sliding them, on long-handled paddles, into a huge stone wood-fired oven." Bread and visiting bakeries became Schulman's passion in later travels to countries in the Mediterranean, though she prefers to eat bread baked in her own oven.

The following morning, I got up very early and went into the still dark kitchen with fresh bread on my mind. The cover of Martha Shulman's book pictured a crusty, round loaf of French country bread. The ingredients and directions were simple. Active dry yeast, lukewarm water, olive oil, whole wheat flour, fresh rosemary and thyme, salt, and unbleached white flour.

By sunrise when Kit came down for breakfast, I had made coffee and fed the barn cats, house cats, our chunky dog, and a flock of geese and ducks. Sitting over the kitchen floor heater vent, a batch of hand-kneaded bread dough was busy doubling in a covered, earthenware bowl. A dusting of King Arthur flour still covered the marble kitchen counter as well as my hands and apron. And above the smell of fresh coffee, the yeasty smell of bread dough on the rise filled the kitchen with our mutual anticipation of tastes to come.

Bakers like my friend Suzanne and Martha Schulman and Poilane believe that their soul is connected to the making of bread. They love the physicality of making bread and the smell of bread baking. But perhaps most of all, bakers love knowing that their bread nourishes the community and they gain fulfillment in seeing their neighbors enjoying the bread.

My own experience with hand made breads has just begun. As I work my flour-covered hands through the recipes of great bakers, I will build meals around country sourdough loaves, foccacia, pizzas, biscuits and yeast breads; and I will invite friends to break bread with us at Breakfast Creek. For as every baker with a passion for bread knows, it is the act of sharing bread that is the bread maker's greatest reward. (1995)

Corn and Tomatoes

Imagine summer without corn and tomatoes. You can't, can you? That would be like thinking about French cuisine without garlic or butter, Irish food without potatoes, or Italian meals without olive oil. Living in the American Heartland, corn and tomatoes are as essential in the recipe for summer as capsicum pepper is to an Indian curry or paprika is to Hungarian goulash.

In the Midwest, corn marks the progress of summer's calendar. In the weeks before the September harvest, a farmer will stop in the early evening on his way home from the fields to pull off an ear of corn, shuck the husk, and study the lines that have grown within. With a slow and careful eye, the farmer reads his future like a fortuneteller reads the palm of a hand.

In Hartsburg, farmers have gotten through July this year without the damaging flood rains that came in '93 and again in '95. The reading this summer is for a bumper crop and high corn prices. With luck, the shiny new grain bins some farmers have been busily adding during August will soon be filled to overflowing. barring some unforeseen disaster, it looks like the '96 corn harvest will be a profitable one.

When Kit and I drove around the Hartsburg Bottoms earlier this summer during the height of the wheat harvest, the corn rows planted right up to the edge of the narrow gravel roads were already over the cab of my truck. We drove amazed through a maze of maize. Tassels had just started to appear when June turned the corner and headed into July. From backyard kitchen gardens, sweet corn and fat, juicy tomatoes find their way to the table just about every meal. In the summertime, nothing tastes better than a plate of thickly sliced, Beefsteak tomatoes accompanied by a few steaming ears of just picked, buttered sweet corn. A little salt and a slice of Barbara Beckmeyer's homemade dill bread to sop up any leftover buttery juices and that, my friends is a meal fit for a queen.

While we are on the subject of queens, look back five centuries to the time of Isabella when there was no chocolate or vanilla in France, no capsicum (chili) pepper in India, no paprika in Hungary, and believe it or not, not a single tomato had ever been seen in an Italian *cuccina* or *trattoria*. Five hundred years ago, these foods—along with potatoes, many kinds of beans, squashes and pumpkins, turkey, pineapple, wild rice, peanuts, and pecans—were found only in the New World. Each of these foods had its own unique history. In the years following the "discovery" of the New World, native North American foods were shared, borrowed, transported great distances across great oceans, and changed in different ways depending on the shore to which each was transported.

In subsequent years, each of these foods found its way into the cuisine of new homelands—in Europe, Asia, Africa, the Middle East, and the Mediterranean where they continued to be refined and cultivated. With immigration to the Americas in the nineteenth and twentieth centuries, the journey of these native foods has come full circle. Gradually, there has been a fusion of flavors from the Old World with the traditional diet of the Heartland. Over time, we've come to deem this melting pot of tastes—from French fries and ketchup, to pizza and Cornflakes—as uniquely American as apple pie.

This morning, I couldn't sit down at the kitchen table because I had tucked four baskets full of tomatoes close to the floor vent to keep the fruit cool. Each day I remind myself that I need to do something with all these tomatoes. That means going to the basement, bringing up the canning jars and equipment, clearing surfaces in the kitchen, boiling pots of water on the stovetop, and putting desk work aside for the day. Several years ago when I first expressed an interest in canning, Barbara Beckmeyer came over for a morning and taught me the secret of canning tomatoes. That morning of first-hand instruction led to the construction of a pantry off our kitchen that is now filled much of the year with tomato sauces and salsas, peach and mango chutneys, brandied peaches, and herbal vinegars.

Most recently, sun-dried tomatoes were added to the panty. Because much of what I create in our kitchen is Mediterranean in spirit and flavor, I often use sun-dried tomatoes packed in virgin olive oil and fresh basil when I am preparing a fresh pasta dish. I also love the way the jars look on a pantry shelf and enjoy giving sun-dried tomatoes as a gift from Breakfast Creek. The drying process is easy.

Sun-dried Tomatoes

- Put tin foil on a cookie sheet. Slice plum tomatoes (I use Romas) and arrange them face up on the cookie sheet.
- Sprinkle the tomatoes with kosher salt and "dry" them in a very slow oven (200°) overnight, or for approximately 12 hours.
- When the tomatoes look dry, pack them in a sterilized jar, add several fresh basil leaves, and cover them with virgin olive oil. Add a sprig of rosemary.
- Then seal the jar and store these sun-filled treasures in your pantry.

Kit loves a bowl of hot tomato soup for lunch when the weather turns cool. Interestingly enough, I have never tried to turn our abundant harvest of Roma tomatoes into a good old-fashioned basic homemade tomato soup. This summer, I may try to emulate John T. Dorrance, the New Jersey chemist who a century ago set the standard for tomato soup for generations of Americans to come. New Jersey, for all the bad press it gets today, is still the Garden State, rich in truck farms and tomatoes. With the birth of the New Jersey chemist's condensed product, Campbell's Tomato Soup, Americans got their first taste of his distinctive, slightly sweet and cinnamon-spiced soup.

Even earlier, Heinz had bottled catsup in sturdy glass bottles, perhaps anticipating the forthcoming popularity of the American hot dog. And though the glass bottle has been replaced by plastic squeeze bottles and "catsup" is now "ketchup," Heinz claims that its 120-year-old original recipe has remained basically the same. Kit and our friend, Larry Hall, are mighty relieved. Along with peanut butter, Kit's favorite food, he holds ketchup up there with the finest *au jus* and steak sauces. Larry likes his ketchup straight—spread on your basic white bread and eaten as a sandwich. When ordering a steak at Trattoria Strata Nova, currently our favorite Italian restaurant in Columbia, Kit is not shy about asking for a side dish of "the magic sauce." Ketchup is smuggled to our table in a small dish, without the "k" word ever being mentioned to Michael Odette, the *trattoria's* wonderful chef.

I prefer diversity and experimentation when it comes to ordering foods made from tomatoes and corn. Forget the ketchup. I'll take sun-dried tomato pesto or tomato chutney for my relish. When there is no longer fresh corn on the cob available, I might cook up a pot of polenta (*Grits Milanese*), or try the recipe that I have just found for corn and shrimp fritters, Thai style.

The combinations and possibilities for preparing corn and tomatoes are endless. They taste their sweetest and finest on the palette when fresh and served without fuss. When summer ends and it is time to head for the pantry or freezer, we will continue to enjoy the flavors that are so close to our hearts and stomachs these days. Heritage foods of the Heartland passed down through the ages from the Old World to our table at Breakfast Creek. Sweet corn and sliced tomatoes. Plain and simply delicious. (1996)

Comforting Thoughts

Sunday morning began with predictions of icy rain and treacherous driving conditions. A public radio announcement followed by phone calls and an e-mail message from friends in Hartsburg brought word that church had been called off. The fear was that ice on Nichols Hill leading in and out of town would make it treacherous at the very time parishioners would be heading home.

With that, Kit fed the barn animals and brought up a few armloads of firewood. While he got a fire going and made a pot of coffee, I fried some eggs and bacon. It looked like we would be spending an entire day of unexpected house arrest at Breakfast Creek. There would actually be time to read the whole Sunday paper, sip a leisurely cup of coffee, keep a fire going continuously, and slowly simmer a pot roast all afternoon long. What a comforting thought!

In the Midwest, you never know what January will bring. Sunday's predicted ice never materialized. In fact that very afternoon, a bluebird arrived at one of the hanging feeders visible from our kitchen window. After verifying my sighting with a pair of binoculars, I asked myself: What blessed breeze had brought nature's loveliest harbinger of spring to Breakfast Creek before January has departed the scene?

The optimist in me would like to think that the bluebird's arrival is a sign of an early spring. Then I remember the plight of the South Dakota farmer. Up there, winter keeps dumping fresh snow onto drifts that are by now higher than some of the farmhouses. The concerns are real and immediate—clearing buried roads, locating stranded drivers, and getting feed to farm animals. Even the old timers with long memories are beginning to talk about this being the worst winter they can remember, and it is a long way from being over.

When I was a senior in high school, my family moved from northern Virginia to Nebraska. It was a move that I likened to Siberian exile in daily letters written over that winter to the friends I had left back east. That same winter, Dad was caught in a snowstorm while driving between Lincoln and Omaha and ended up spending the night at a farmhouse along with a number of other stranded motorists. Luckily for all, the house had a well-stocked freezer. While we worried at home about Dad's whereabouts, he was enjoying the comforts of a generous table filled with all-American, down home, warm-your-innards comfort food.

This may be one of those winters when those of us who live in the country find ourselves digging deeper and deeper into our freezers and pantry reserves. Each time winter bites, I find myself searching for comfort in nostalgic memories of childhood mealtime favorites. Searching that distant reservoir, I am warmed by comforting thoughts of familiar foods I have loved since childhood when Mother served them to our family in the 1950s.

Monday morning, we again awoke to reports of freezing rain on its way. The day sounded like a weathercaster's dream. Icy rain all morning, followed by sleet and 3–4 inches of snow by late afternoon. Smoothly, the Doppler weather wizard presented his most dire forecast. "Bad ..." he pronounced in gleeful sound bites, "... messy ... getting worse ... temperatures plummeting ... lows of zero to minus 5° ... wind chills of 20°-30° below."

Icy roads terrify me. When Kit drove off that morning just ahead of the freezing rain, I recalled a scene from Michael Ondaatje's novel *The English Patient* when Katherine and Count Almásy take haven in a truck just as a sand storm envelops the North African desert around them. "This isn't good, is it?" says Katherine. "No, it is not," Almásy responds, wiping the sand from his face. "Shall we be all right?" Katherine asks with a tone of concern. "Yes." Almásy answers. "Yes.... Absolutely." To which Katherine responds, "*Yes* is a comfort. *Absolutely* is not."

As predicted, icy rain fell all that morning. By noon the cedars were bent and groaned under the crushing weight of their crystal coats. It was a wintery scene from *Doctor Zhivago*. Rain fell frozen against the windows. The sharp ping of glass striking glass. Finding no comfort in the scene outside, I searched my memory for a warm and comforting dish from Mother's kitchen. The perfect homey food, guaranteed to melt the heart and warm the spirit. Finally, it came to me. Homemade macaroni and cheese.

Mother's baked macaroni and cheese recipe, I recalled, had come from her 1955 vintage copy of *The Good Housekeeping Cookbook*. My own edition of the same book was published in 1963—the same year that I graduated from high school after surviving my first Nebraska winter. I compared her recipe with one from Diane Rossen Worthington's 1995 cookbook, *Diner: The Best of Casual American Cooking*. They were almost identical.

It is dark now and quite cold outside. Inside, a fire is blazing in the fireplace and the barn light is on to welcome Kit home. In the oven, a dish of old fashioned macaroni and cheese is baking up a storm. Comfort food for an icy January night. A comforting connection that never fails to take me back home. (1997)

Macaroni and Cheese

MACARONI: 1 tsp. salt + 2 1/2 cups of elbow macaroni boiled rapidly for 5–7 minutes. Drain, rinse in cold water to remove excess starch, and drizzle with 1 Tbs. olive oil. Set aside.

SAUCE: In a saucepan over medium-low heat, combine 3 tbs. butter + 3 tbs. flour, whisking until bubbly and golden. Gradually add 2 1/2 cups milk, simmer until smooth and slightly thickened, 3–4 mins. Add 1 3/4 cups Cheddar cheese to the milk, remove from heat, and add 1/2 tsp. each of salt and pepper, 2 tsp. Dijon mustard, and 1 tsp. chopped parsley. Pour sauce over macaroni, mix, and transfer to a buttered baking dish.

TOPPING: 3/4 cup Cheddar cheese + 1/2 cup fresh breadcrumbs + 1tsp. butter.

BAKE: 20–25 minutes at 375º. [Serves 4 comfortably.]

American Pie

A year ago, I made my first lemon meringue pie. Having reached the half-century mark, I figured that it was about time that I find out the deep and rich secret to making meringue that my mother mastered when I was a child. I never thought to ask her for a recipe for her heavenly lemon pies when I set up my own household. I copied her recipes for meatloaf, pecan pie, cornbread turkey stuffing, and homemade barbecue sauce, but meringue remained in a category impossibly akin to clouds and angels. Only a chosen few, it seemed to me then, could make a pie that mirrored a cloud burnt by sunlight. When it came to Mom's meringue, she was in the company of angels.

In my library of cookbooks, I browsed through one that was a collection of the best of roadside diner food. This was the food of common people, served in roadside establishments that drew on America's romance with the old Pullman dining cars of the 1920s. Their comforting fare came at a bargain price, making diners affordable even in the leanest years of the Great Depression. By the 1950s, such eating spots were an American institution. We were a nation on the move in brand new automobiles painted apple pie á la mode colors. Diners fueled mobile Americans filled with postwar optimism, a sense of prosperity, and an appetite for living.

Reading through the Diner cookbook, I learned that—like the American diner—this heavenly dessert is itself a kind of American tradition. While pastry shells filled with lemon curd can be traced back to European kitchens, topping the lemon filling with meringue is as American as, well, apple pie, dating from the 1800s. Custard pies came out of kitchens in the pre-cholesterol conscious days when Americans ate eggs with abandon. The filling is a carefully blended and cooked mixture of sugar, cornstarch, salt, water, egg yolks (4), butter, and fresh lemon juice. The meringue is the stuff of air. Egg whites (5) and cream of tartar whipped into peaks, with a dash of sugar and salt. Then, more vigorous beating until finally stiff peaks can be formed with the back of a spoon.

The recipe warned me that every ingredient should be measured ahead and be at the ready. When the filling finally thickens and is poured hot into a pre-baked pie shell, the moment for meringue arrives. The beater hits the egg whites and the cook evokes the angels, praying for miraculous transformations of air and water into snow-capped peaks. Four minutes later, a mountain of meringue is piled onto the still hot lemon filling, peaks are pushed even higher with the back of a spoon, and the pie is put in a moderate oven for 12–15 minutes until the meringue's peaks and moraines turn golden as if burnt by the sun.

I had decided to make the pie because it was Memorial Day weekend. The morning before, I had been in our garden when chapters of aviation history passed directly overhead, including a B-17, B-25 Mitchell, and a P-51—all planes from earlier wars and eras collecting for the local air show. I immediately went to the phone and called my father in San Antonio. "You won't believe what just flew over Breakfast Creek," I said. "A B-17 and a B-25!"

Dad flew both of theses planes early in his 30-year career as an Air Force pilot. Those were the years when Mother often looked upward for strength, praying for Dad's safe return. It was a time when much of her attention was focused on caring for their two little girls—my sister Molly and me. I don't know exactly when Mother decided to attempt her first lemon meringue pie. She'd never even fried bacon before marrying my father in 1942.

Dad on the other hand, grew up in a large family and was raised in Pennsylvania on a dairy farm. During the long months of separation in the final years of WWII, Mother may have looked for a lemon meringue pie recipe, knowing it was one of Dad's favorites.

She now claims that the recipe I remember from my childhood days came from her copy of Marsh's 1955 *Good Housekeeping Cookbook*—now a vintage classic selling for $58.00 in B-condition. To this day, it remains her favorite cookbook.

On the Monday morning that Memorial Day is observed, I listened to a rousing selection of patriotic music for marching bands on National Public Radio. Leonard Slatkin and the St. Louis Symphony set the stage for a reading of Lincoln's "Gettysburg Address" by General Norman Schwartzkoff. It was a powerful hour that brought back the historic meaning of Memorial Day. A day of remembrance. A day when American families and veterans go to cemeteries around the country to decorate the graves of veterans of foreign wars and military service.

In my garden later that morning, I moved slowly up and down the rows of peas and strawberries. It was a quiet place to think about this most American of days. I imagined cemeteries across the country, row after straight row of small American flags by stones marking the memory of the American veterans—brave sons and daughters, brothers and sisters, fathers and mothers, who gave their lives in the service of their country.

In Hartsburg's Friedens Evangelical Cemetery, local veterans and their families collect every Memorial Day to honor both living and deceased friends and relatives who defended democracy in World War I, World War II, the Korean War, the Vietnam War, the Gulf War, Somalia, and Bosnia. It is a town with a long history of service to its community, its two churches and to its country. Here, patriotism is still something to be proud of and talked about.

After the Memorial Day service at the American Legion Hall in Hartsburg, veterans and their families gather to share memories and a meal together. Most likely, the menu this year will be country fare—fried chicken, baked potatoes, green beans, homemade rolls, apple butter, and a selection of homemade pies. Apple, rhubarb and strawberry, and perhaps even a lemon meringue pie.

This food is symbolic of home. Of what wars are supposed to be all about. Democracy and keeping the world safe for our children and grandchildren. So that our treasured American heritage can be passed on to the next generation. For these reasons, I am enormously grateful for the years of service of my grandfathers, my Uncle Bud, and my father who was a pilot in the Pacific Theater during WWII. I am especially thoughtful of these sacrifices on Memorial Day and I buy red crepe paper poppies made for the occasion by local veterans. Then I bake a lemon meringue pie in honor of my mother, Alice and all the mothers who kept our homes and world in balance all those years ago. (1996)

Garam Masala

When Aliya found herself back in Pakistan, she had just turned thirteen. Now at twenty-six, this beautiful young woman is eagerly embracing life once again in America. Her story has been a poignant journey, one she recounted recently during her first visit to Breakfast Creek. While memories still bring pain, her life is finally her own. For this dear niece of mine, freedom is experienced each day through the simplest of acts—mailing a letter, riding in a taxi, making a phone call, or expressing an opinion.

Aliya's eyes reflect a world that I know of, but have never experienced first hand. In the hours that we talked during her visit, her large, dark eyes never once lost their focus as we spoke. Their intensity became a screen on which her words were projected. And much of the time, we held hands to remind ourselves that she was really home again.

When Aliya arrived recently with my nephew Adam and their mother, Kim (my sister), we quickly fell into a pattern of cooking together in the kitchen. Aliya and Kim moved in a harmony that needed few words. Theirs is a love that has survived years of separation, and now the simple act of cooking together is an event of the greatest joy. This is the story of a traditional Pakistani meal prepared in the kitchen at Breakfast Creek during their visit.

On the designated day of curry creation, Aliya produced a packet of prepared *Garam masala* that she had brought from Nepal where she lived with my sister, Molly, in the months just preceding her return to the United States. With future curries already in mind, I made certain that each of the individual ingredients that goes into the *masala* was on hand in my collection of spices. We were, as they say, in business!

Garam masala, traditionally used in northern Indian cuisine, means literally "warm spice blend." Its spices are supposed to heat the body. In the South Asian region of India and Pakistan and in areas of the Middle East, it is stirred into curries and pilafs toward the end of cooking.

> ## Garam Masala
>
> To make your own *Garam masala*, blend the following ground spices:
>
> - 1 tablespoon cardamom, 2 1/2 teaspoons coriander, 2 teaspoons cumin, 1 teaspoon black pepper, 1/2 teaspoon cloves, 1/2 teaspoon cinnamon, and 1/2 teaspoon nutmeg.
> - If you have a mortar and pestle, grind the whole spices after dry-roasting them in a hot pan over low heat.

It was decided that we would make two traditional Pakistani dishes—*keema* (a spicy ground beef dish) and chicken curry. Both would be served with Basmati rice, freshly sliced mangoes and pineapple, a condiment of yogurt mixed with diced cucumber, black pepper and salt called *raita*, and finally, peach and mango chutney from our pantry at Breakfast Creek. There were onions to be sliced, chicken to be chopped, garlic to be crushed, tomatoes to be cubed, ginger to be diced and cilantro to be collected from the herb garden.

Kim's assignment was the *keema*. Aliya prepared the chicken curry. I was given the tearful task of chopping onions that made taking notes during the preparation stages of the meal impossible. "Dear Aliya," I said through my tears, "I will happily chop onions all afternoon if you will promise to sit down later and write out both recipes for me."

For the next hour, the three of us worked as one in the small area around the stovetop in the kitchen. In a large pan, Kim cooked a small, thinly sliced onion in 2 tablespoons of oil, stirring until it was golden brown. She then added 4 cloves of crushed garlic and a pound of ground beef, stirring until the meat turned a light brown. To this, she added, 2 teaspoons of *Garam masala*, salt, 3 cubed tomatoes, and one cup of peas, stirring for 2–3 minutes before adding a second small, thinly sliced onion and one teaspoon of finely sliced ginger. Finally, chopped cilantro leaves were added. With the flame turned up, Kim stirred the mixture until the keema was sufficiently dry.

In a pot on another burner, Aliya cooked a large, thinly sliced onion in 2 tablespoons of oil until it was golden brown. She then added 3 cloves of crushed garlic and 3 cut up chicken breasts, cooking them until slightly tender. In a bowl, I mixed 3 tablespoons of plain yogurt with *Garam masala*, which we added along with two chopped tomatoes and salt to the chicken mixture.

By now, the smell of the "warm spice blend" had transformed the kitchen into a Pakistani *rasoi* (kitchen). For ten minutes, the mixture simmered until the chicken became tender, the juices of the tomatoes had been released, and the liquid was reduced to a thick *kari* (sauce). To complete the curry, Aliya added a teaspoon of finely sliced ginger and a generous helping of chopped cilantro leaves, stirring continuously for another 2 minutes. Both dishes were then ready to be removed from the fire and served with Basmati rice, the *raita,* and other assorted condiments.

That evening's meal filled us with the flavors of *keema* and *kari*. But more than that, we had renewed our own *masala* of mother and daughter, niece and aunt, and sisters. A rich family blend more precious than saffron, one guaranteed to warm the heart. (1997)

Chapter Six

Family

A Solid Citizen

Beginning in 1945

Backyards

A Wing and a Prayer

Auctions and Families Past

The Girls

Nicolás

A Solid Citizen

Handing down family stories is a way of remembering where we come from and knowing who we are. I have gone to such stories in search of my roots as the granddaughter of a farmer. The story begins and ends with a dance. My parents met at a dance at the Gunter Hotel in San Antonio. She was the daughter of an army officer. He was a young pilot in the Army Air Corps, the son of a West Virginia dairy farmer. It was 1941 and young men like my father had been drawn from colleges and farms around the country to train for overseas duty. They were introduced that evening, and Mother went home with news that she had "met the most beautiful man." "Granny," she said, describing my father to my great grandmother, "he's a solid citizen." Indeed, when Great Granny met him, she agreed that he was.

Dad was the youngest of seven children. His oldest sister had already begun her family of eleven children when Dad was born in 1918. Though I never met my paternal grandparents, Elza and Mary Dague Riggs, I grew up with stories about Dad's brothers, Harry, Robert, Ralph, and Lloyd; his sisters, Hazel and Pansey; his cousins, Easter and Elizabeth, who were like sisters to my father; and Uncle Charlie, a bachelor uncle who lived with Dad's family. From an old picture of the farmhouse and some of their Jersey cows, I have come to know the Springdale Dairy Farm in West Finley, West Virginia. That is where Dad and Uncle Ralph were born. Dad is the little boy in the 1922 Chevy parked in front of the house in a black and white photograph that sits on my father's bureau.

My grandfather lost the West Virginia farm in 1929, but managed to move the cows and farm equipment by train at night to Bedford, Pennsylvania, and drive the herd to a small farm he had bought five miles out of town. Dad attended 4th grade in a one-room schoolhouse near the farm and remembers the Depression years as a time when the family had "lots to eat, but no money." Farming supported their growing dairy herd. Milk sold to a dairy in Bedford was turned into cash needed to continually upgrade the farm. By the time Dad had reached high school, the family had been able to buy a larger farm with 25 dairy cows, two teams of draft horses, and tractors for working the corn, oats, wheat, and hay crops needed for silage during the winter months.

When my father entered college in 1938, FDR's Rural Electrification Program had begun, but it would take years to reach their farm. Milk was cooled by massive blocks of ice cut from the creek and covered with sawdust in the icehouse. Canning, kitchen pantries, iceboxes, and cool cellars all took the place of refrigeration. A steer was killed in the fall, the meat cut up, boiled, and stored in half-gallon cold packed canning jars in the cellar. Limas, green beans, peas, carrots, and tomatoes were put up, and upward of 200 quarts of blackberries would be cold packed in their own juices with sugar.

Fall was also hog butchering time. On day one, 10–12 hogs were butchered, boiled, hung, and scraped clean. After airing out for several hours, they were cut into shoulders, tenderloins, hocks, and bacon slabs. Another section was rendered into lard the following day. In the same big black kettles used to boil the hogs, fat was boiled out. Solid pieces of fat were pressed into lard cakes, while liquid fat solidified like Crisco and was stored in lard cans in the cellar.

Next, the hogs' heads were cooked and the lean meat cut out for "cheese," ground up, and stored in crocks in the cellar. Hogshead broth, the ground meat, and corn meal were fried into scrapple. When cold, the "cheese" was sliced and fried like corn meal mush. At the end of day one of the fall butchering, the family would eat fried liver, and the loin would be eaten soon after while still fresh. Other meat—the hams, shoulders, and bacon—was cured.

Curing was done over a period of several days in the cellar or a shed. The meat from four or five hogs was put on sawhorses. Handfuls of salt, brown sugar and pepper were rubbed and packed on hams and the meat to draw out the water. The meat was then taken to the smokehouse and hung for a week from rafters over a hickory fire. My grandmother wrapped the dried and hickory-cured meat in cotton sacking, and the hams continued to hang through the winter, spring, summer, and into the next fall. She would cut meat from a ham as the family needed it and then hang it back in the cellar.

Sausage was made from trimmings left over when the hog meat was shaped into the various cuts. After being put through a sausage grinder, sage dressing was added. The sausage meat was then packed into 5-gallon earthen crocks with wooden lids and stored in the cellar. For breakfast sausage, my grandmother scooped sausage into a bowl and shaped it into patties. Since there was no refrigeration other than an icebox, the sausage had to be used up during cold weather.

Fall on the farm was a busy time because it was also harvest season. Wheat was cut with a reaper pulled by draft horses. My grandfather loved Morgan horses and always saw himself as a horseman. For that reason, he never did learn to drive. After the reaper cut the wheat and packed it into sheaths wrapped with twine, the sheaths were gathered by hand into shocks of wheat, pitched onto a large flat bed wagon and driven into the upper part of the barn where they were stacked.

At this time, my grandfather would arrange for threshers to come and notified the other farmers who then came to help. Threshing was generally a one-day operation, and on those days, the local women came to help with the cooking. A noon meal was served outside—meat (beef), ham, potatoes, dumplings, bread and rolls, pies, cakes, iced tea, lemonade, coffee and milk. By 5 p.m., the farmers would return to their own farms to milk their cows. Farming involved the whole family as well as the whole community.

My father grew from these strong roots to be a solid citizen. I see the same qualities and work ethic in the farming community where Kit and I now live in central Missouri. The Great Flood of '93 has made the community an even stronger family than it was before. Rebuilding continues seven months after the floods, and through it all, the Hartsburg community has kept its spirit alive. Every two months, locals come to a dinner dance at the American Legion Hall in town and for five hours dance the night away. I feel at home surrounded by farms and farmers. The solid citizens of this small Missouri town are my neighbors and my friends. Through them, I have gained a window into a world much like the one my father knew as a boy, and I have started to dance again. Though much about the nature of farming has changed over the years, farm life continues to provide a solid foundation from which to view the world and celebrate the nature of family. (1994)

Beginning in 1945

Life magazine has called 1945 the century's watershed year. In that year, according to *Life*, "the world as we know it was born." For me, truer words were never spoken, though I didn't appear on the scene until the third week of October—understandably, my favorite month ever since. For fifty years now, I have had 1945 as my reference point and growth marker for measuring the distances I have traveled from where my life began. For me, it still seems like just the other day.

As I was beginning my journey in October 1945, what was going on in America and the world? Almost unbelievably, Mussolini, Hitler, and Roosevelt all died in the same month. Americans heard the words Auschwitz, Belsen, Dachau, and Buchenwald for the first time. Hollywood let Americans escape from it all. Humphrey Bogart, 46, married a beautiful 20-year-old actress named Lauren Bacall. For a brief moment, *Life* magazine reminds us, America believed again in rainbows.

As the war went on in Europe and the Pacific, Americans at home shared in the pain. Housewives (Kitchen Commandos) did their best with less. Less meat, more homegrown fruits and vegetables. More than 20 million people planted "victory gardens" which accounted for a third of America's vegetable harvest in 1945. Hamburgers were actually veggie burgers made with oatmeal, eggs, onions and sage. Macaroni went cheeseless with tomato sauce; and, of course, there was Spam.

Ration stamps took the place of dollars, and recycling—all but forgotten after the war—was a passion with American kids in 1945. When Bing Crosby sang, "Junk will win the war," children collected scrap metal, coat hangers, worn-out rubber, paper, and even fat (for explosives) as their contribution to the war effort.

America in 1945 saw the beginning of a social revolution that has matured along with my own growth over the past half century. The hope and promise for equality in the workplace and society that women and blacks felt they earned during the war years did not happen quickly.

By the time I graduated from high school, Martin Luther King had given a charismatic voice to the civil rights movement. As an eighteen-year-old college student, I went by myself to a church in Lincoln, Nebraska to hear Reverend King speak. His message about the need for racial harmony and a kinder humanity left me uncomfortably aware of how monochromatic my experiences in the world had been up to that time, something I have worked to change ever since.

In 1970, fifty years after women gained the right to vote, Women's Liberation was a movement with new voices and energy. Women, the voices said, "had come a long way, Baby"; from the popular belief in 1945 that a woman's place was in the kitchen. I have always felt selfishly glad that my sisters and I had a mother who chose to be a homemaker, but I realize now what a personal sacrifice it was on her part. She could have been a model, a terrific businesswoman, an interior decorator, or anything she set her sharp and creative mind to. Instead, she made the world happen for her four girls and created a stable home on solid ground wherever our frequent moves with the Air Force took us over the years.

America, too, has come a long way since 1945, and yet that progress is often ambiguous. In a year (1995) when some Americans are seriously considering a man of color for president, 40 percent of America's black children still live in poverty. In 1995, America is divided along racial lines. Women have made tremendous progress in the workplace, but as yet, rarely make it to the top positions in business and politics. Social progress has been made, but we've still got miles to go.

When WW II ended, progress couldn't be held back. The nation, notes *Life*, was ready to build, spend money on tankfuls of gas and superhighways, move to the suburbs, and fill their new houses with laborsaving devices. With the explosion of supermarkets that followed the war, it was no longer necessary for women busy with children and careers to plant victory gardens and spend days preserving provender for the winter months.

Over the past fifty years, neighborhood grocery stores have been largely replaced by supermarkets, mega markets, and one-stop Wal-Mart Super Centers where you can shop, service your car, fill a prescription, have film developed, and grab a quick bite to eat. Shelves are filled with products that aim to make cooking easy and faster, so that busy women, and now, increasingly men, can be in and out of the kitchen in record time. Sauces come premixed, frozen dinners can be microwaved in a matter of minutes, and dieters can mix up a liquid meal in only seconds.

The irony is that half a century after they were a national necessity, I have discovered the joys of a kitchen garden and a pantry filled with produce I have harvested and canned myself. I enjoy making bread and pie crust from scratch. Mother was a wonderful cook, though she claims not to have known how to even fry bacon when she married my father. Her gray covered Good Housekeeping cookbook was her kitchen aide when I was ten years old—and it is still a part of her kitchen today. Dog-eared and food-stained from more than fifty years of continuous use, it remains her favorite cookbook today.

America has spent a great deal of time this year looking back at the events of 1945. D-Day. The bombing of Hiroshima and Nagasaki. V-J Day. I knew about these events, studied them in school, and talked about them with my own students when I was a teacher. But it is only now, fifty years later, that I have come to fully appreciate those events and the role my father, younger then than my own son is now, played as a pilot in the Pacific theater.

This year, those who fought in the final battles in Europe and the Pacific just months before I was born, finally shared their stories and feelings about their experiences, collectively buried all these years by the 'greatest generation.' Veterans returned to battle sites in Europe or the Pacific for the first time in half a century. There, they found new worlds and sought to lay old ghosts to rest. It had been a patriotic war, a war to save the world from evil. When it ended, people put the war behind them and moved on.

In 1945, Rocky Graziano was Boxer of the Year. Gertrude Stein died. John Hersey wrote *Hiroshima,* and Dr. Benjamin Spock wrote *Baby and Child Care.* Robert E. Byrd explored the South Pole. Women gained the right to vote in France, and a year later in Italy. *Brigadoon* opened on Broadway. Popular songs included "How Are Things in Gloccamorra?" "Tenderly," "Zip-a-dee-doo-dah," and "Come Rain or Come Shine." St. Louis won the World Series 4 games to 3 by defeating Boston. America was ready to bebop, and so was I. On October 21, 1945 I joined the ranks of America's baby boomers. Three days later, the United Nations was formed to keep the world of my childhood at peace.

This is the setting for my story … beginning in 1945. It is a snapshot of what *Life* described as the year "the world as we know it was born." Certain parts of the picture I remember because I was there. Others I have learned at different ages as an observer of the times. What is missing are the chapters of the stories from those years that include my family, experiences as a teacher and a writer, travels, friendships, and my life with Kit. Their stories fill the inner chapters as well as those still being written as my life approaches the half-century mark. 1945 was only the beginning. (1995)

Backyards

Each year as May slips quietly into June, fireflies turn the pastures around Breakfast Creek into fields of miniature lanterns, and I am a child again. I stop, amazed at the miracle of light stored in the bodies of these small flying insects, electrified by the force of such energy dancing all around me. These magic fields become the backyards of my past and the fireflies are a thousand Tinkerbells carrying me back to the places where I played as a child.

Each of us has a personal collection of mental maps of the backyards of our lives. No two collections are the same and no two people emerge from their childhood backyards shaped by exactly the same experiences. Each map delineates a place or experience that touched us in our growing up. Like the energy stored by a firefly, they generate a reflection on who we have become.

My earliest backyard lay just beyond the kitchen door. It was a safe, grass-covered place that my bare-footed sisters and I shared with a silky-coated cocker spaniel and toys that kept our imaginations busy during the hours that we spent there. As we grew, the space we played in spilled over into the yards of our friends.

During the summer between second and third grade, evenings were filled with the magic of storytelling. Summer nights in Fort Worth, in the years before air conditioning, drove us into the backyard where storytelling was the pastime of adults and children alike. My parents gathered with friends around hurricane lanterns telling stories filled with grownup words that delighted me and names that became part of the family story I was beginning to construct in my eight-year old head. Across the street, my sisters and I sat on the front lawn with Tom and Billy Shields telling ghost stories and fighting wars with grass spears. We had no lanterns—only fireflies to illuminate the darkening sky and help us find our way home when the stories and battles came to an end.

When I was nine and ten we lived in a circle of base housing at Westover Air Force Base in western Massachusetts. Traditional front yards faced inward creating a grassy common within the circle of houses—a sprawling, communal playground for neighborhood children of all ages.

Each winter, the circle was intentionally flooded to create a community skating rink where we spent all of the hours that we were not in school. With a small transistor radio tucked into my back pocket, I patiently practiced skating backwards and imagined myself skating from that backyard rink into the world of the Ice Capades. We played ice hockey with brooms from our mothers' kitchens and never tired or complained of being cold. Those were times that built strong ankles, demanded disciplined bladders, and kept our cheeks rosy. The covered porch outside our kitchen was always filled with snow boots and wet snow suits. And in the kitchen, marshmallows melted by the thousands in the cups of hot chocolate that warmed us up once we finally answered Mother's, or nature's, call to come inside.

As a twenty-one year old teaching in Thailand, my backyard was bordered by a canal that ran past a nearby Buddhist monastery. My small, two-story framed house had no screens on the windows and its proximity to the canal presented a very real challenge each evening. In that tropical world of giant mosquitoes, I never once was able to sit on my open back stoop to read or watch the spectacular sunsets that arrived each evening in shades of pink and lavender. Instead, I was forced to retire to my room upstairs and push open the wooden shutters that sealed the room from assorted flying and crawling creatures during the day. Sitting at my desk in front of the unscreened window that looked out on the monastery, I would light a mosquito coil balanced on the neck of a coke bottle and place it near my feet. From that window, I watched the sun set behind monks as they washed their saffron-colored robes and hung them in the warm evening air to dry. When the coil had burned to its end, I was forced to duck under my mosquito net for the night, wishing that mosquitoes were fireflies and backyards from my past weren't so far away.

Over the past twenty years, my travels have afforded me a window into backyards distant and diverse from those of my own childhood. In Los Angeles, our backyard was an urban canyon still wild with chaparral, raccoons and coyotes. In Washington, D.C., it was a small brick patio reclaimed from a narrow alley, shared with our two rarely used small cars. Trips with Kit to various regions of Europe and China, as well as my earlier travels throughout Asia have given me a sense of how differently people around the world use space. For those fortunate enough to have land attached to a house, life spills outside and we are given space to grow in and secret gardens to create. For others growing up in spaces defined by urban crowding, the city itself is one extended backyard. Streetlights take the place of fireflies, and stars can only be seen on hot summer nights when power overloads lead to brownouts.

Walls around the medieval city of Sienna in Italy surround a maze of cobbled streets with ornate doors leading into interior courtyards, creating worlds within worlds, each separated farther from the Tuscan landscape that lies beyond the city itself. On another scale, backyards are the places that lie just beyond a country's borders. In some cases, we cross easily from one country to the next. In other cases, barriers—some natural, some of human design—serve to keep certain people out and others in.

At Breakfast Creek, the only barriers are the natural flow of berry patches and iris rows. Animals, birds, and humans alike cross freely from field to pond and yard to meadow. Spaces are shared, and it is understood that territories established by one critter are freely traversed by others. Indeed, when the hungry red fox sneaks down to the duck pond, it truly is a jungle out there. A lot of life goes on right here in our backyard. Every day that I am away from it, I know that I am missing some of nature's little dramas. And every night in May that I spend under an urban sky in some distant part of the world, I think about the fireflies that light up the night in the fields that surround Breakfast Creek. (1994)

A Wing and a Prayer

I have only run out of gas once in my thirty-plus years of driving. Three years ago, when my red Chevy pickup truck was still brand new, my father came for a visit. Part of the fun of showing off a new truck is driving old back roads with dips and rolls that years ago inspired someone to describe them as "ribbons of highway." Interstates and new highways have taken the thrill out of the terrain by straightening and leveling the long and winding roads that used to follow the natural flow of the landscape.

Route WW east of Columbia was part the old National Road that later became U.S. 40, the first transcontinental road for automobiles in the United States. This two-lane country road evokes some of the sense of the original game trails American travel followed early on. These natural paths did not follow the compass, but rather the annual migrations of animals back and forth through passes in mountains, across rivers, into rich pastures, and to the best salt springs along the route.

What would be more fun, I thought, than taking my Dad for a spin in my new truck on a leg of the first modern highway to span the state and connect two of America's great inland rivers? We would head out East Broadway onto Daniel Boone's old beaten, now macadamized path, feeling the roll of the road beneath our wheels.

And that is exactly what we did. Route WW winds through pretty horse-farm country and eventually leads to Millersburg. Halfway between my last chance for a gas station in Columbia and my next one in Millersburg, the truck bucked, pitched, and gradually rolled to a complete stop.

Never having run out of gas, I didn't have a clue what had happened. The gas pump icon on my dashboard had not come on to warn me that I was low on fuel; and in my excitement to explore new country roads, I had failed to note that my gas gauge was dangerously close to empty.

My father, on the other hand, *had* run out of gas before, because he responded to my befuddled look with total calm and the simple observation, "Honey, you're out of gas."

"Out of gas?" I blurted out in disbelief. "I can't be out of gas! I'm 45 years old, for Pete's sake. How can I be out of gas?"

There we were, on a less traveled, two-lane, winding ribbon of Missouri country road, five miles from the nearest gas station. It was clearly time for self-reliance and a plan of attack. I would leave Dad by the truck to flag down one of the infrequent passing vehicles while I knocked on the doors of the few houses nearby. It was late afternoon. No one was home and no one seemed to be heading home. For some uncomfortable minutes, a ten-mile round trip walk to get gas was looking like my only remaining option.

And then, a friendly neighbor arrived. A local dad, driving a carpool load of school children home (my first clue to his sainthood status), volunteered to drive out of his way to the nearest gas station in Millersburg. Not only that, he agreed to wait while I fashioned a funnel out of a brown paper bag and filled a plastic gallon-size pickle jar with enough gas to get my truck back to the gas station. He then backtracked five miles to where my father was waiting in my truck. Saint Christopher, patron saint of travelers, had surely been driving the Route WW carpool shift that afternoon.

Luckily, I had had the wit to bring my makeshift paper funnel along so we were able to transfer gas from the plastic pickle jar into the empty tank of my truck. It was embarrassing, but mostly, it was funny. Dad had taught me to drive when I was fifteen; and now, here he was back in the passenger seat thirty years later, teaching me a lesson in self-reliance. The following is a story he told me later that same afternoon about his own ride with Saint Christopher in the year I was born.

In 1945, Dad and the B-29 crew he was piloting were trying to return to their base on Guam after a nighttime bombing run somewhere over Japan. Their plane and Dad's bombardier had been badly shot up, the landing gear was gone, and they were running dangerously low on fuel. Dad was preparing the crew to bail out when a voice over the radio told them of a Japanese-built dirt runway on Iwo Jima, recently secured by the U.S. Marines and Navy. With Saint Christopher watching over his shoulder and God as his co-pilot, Dad executed his first-ever radar-assisted GCA (blind landing), floating safely in on a wing and a prayer—past Mt. Suribachi—a volcano that loomed over the makeshift airstrip.

Gaining access to the Navy's mess tent proved to be more difficult. For understandable reasons, Dad's crew did not have their Army Air Corps dress uniforms along. The U.S. Navy maintained strict dress codes for the officers' mess tent. Unable to talk their way into a hot meal, they resorted to what had carried them to safety—their own self-reliance. They took a last look at their B-29 that would never fly again, dug into their K-rations, and thanked the lucky stars they slept under that night for the new British invention called radar.

Last week, I made my weekly run into Columbia for groceries. I should have gone early in the morning. By late afternoon, the radio announcer was bemoaning the 98° temperatures and explaining why people should never ever leave pets or small children in the car, even for 10 minutes, in such extreme temperatures. I had noted upon leaving Breakfast Creek that the gas gauge was floating around a quarter of a tank and made a mental note to stop at our local Conoco station a mile from home.

Two hours, forty-some miles, and several bags of perishable groceries later, I passed up the opportunity for gas nine miles north of home. Cold air from the truck's air conditioning system was pouring directly onto the grocery bag with the ice cream and butter, and the fuel needle was approaching, but not yet at empty. Just four more miles to our local Conoco station. No need to panic. Then, I detected a slight pull in the engine, and began to consider what I would do if I did run out of gas on Highway 63. Hitchhiking was eliminated right off the bat, I had no car phone, and our neighbors were five or more miles away. I would have to sacrifice the ice cream and walk to the station and back.

That was when the bucking and pitching started in earnest. It really was happening again! I was running out of gas! Instinctively, I shut off the air conditioning and pulled off the highway.

"Honey," I could hear my father saying, "you're out of gas. What are you going to do now?"

I sat for a few very long, hot minutes, collected my rapidly melting confidence, and then tried to start the engine again. Bingo! I traveled two miles closer before it failed again. Then one more brief stop before I made it to the top of the incline that looks down on the Conoco Station. From that elevated point, I rolled on a wing and a prayer down the hill—right into the gas station and up to the first empty gas pump.

I was thankful that I hadn't abandoned the truck or been traveling with small children or pets. I was thankful that Dad had taught me to be level headed in this kind of crisis. And most of all, I was thankful that Saint Christopher had decided to travel south along our stretch of Highway 63 on that particularly hot afternoon. (1994)

Auctions and Families Past

Walking is a balancing act. The foot behind provides the essential balance and push to move the other forward. While our focus in life is mainly on forward progress, it is useful to know where we have been. Looking for the connecting threads that run through our lives, we need to pause occasionally, balancing ourselves on that back foot while we gather up the energy to press ahead.

In the same week, I have lost a friend to cancer and shared in the joy of two births. Each event taken individually stirred powerful emotions in me and caused me to stop moving for a moment. There is a balance that we try to find when bitter and sweet events happen in a close span of time, a connection that might help us understand each event as a piece of a larger whole. Like threads, these events take on meaning when they are connected and ultimately add strength to the fabric that is our lives.

I come away from this week remembering my friend's unflagging optimism and effervescent spirit. Wendy seemed to sparkle and shower friends with positive energy, never dwelling on her illness or bad fortune. Her inner strength enables me to celebrate our friendship and know that it will live long beyond her life itself. When I learn a day later of the birth of little Katie Hobbs, I am moved at the thought of this new little girl who, I am certain, will explore life with the same kind of spirit and curiosity as my friend, Wendy. One balances the other, and I am able to move forward.

Oddly enough, auctions play a similar role in life's balancing act. I went to my first auction soon after moving to Missouri in 1988, but my mother began preparing me for the experience almost half a century ago. In 1955, my parents lived in western Massachusetts. My three sisters and I kept Mother quite busy, but occasionally she managed to slip away on her own to explore local country back roads in search of an auction. Old tobacco barns became the source of antique furniture that Mother brought home and restored to life. We thought she was nothing short of a genius when it came to driving a bargain or spotting a gem amidst the junk.

On road trips in the family's 1955 Chevy station wagon, Mother could smell an auction or junk shop a mile away and was confident she could squeeze almost any bargain into the back of the wagon. That was probably why the back seat was always replaced during family road trips with a mattress. At the time, we thought the mattress was for taking naps and spreading out our toys. Now I know it was to cushion some treasure from the auction that she hoped was underway just around the next bend in the road.

I was drawn to my first auction in Missouri by the words "old quilts" in an announcement in the *Boone County Journal*—Ashland's local weekly newspaper. I went alone, wishing that I had been curious enough forty years earlier to tag along with Mother to some of her tobacco barn auctions. I was in unfamiliar territory, surrounded by people and objects that, like the previous owner, would be gone by the end of the day. My strategy was to quietly browse for awhile, watch what everyone else was doing, let my ear get attuned to the auctioneer's curious jargon, then ease into the bidding while they were auctioning off items under $5.00. When auctioneers changed, I had to adjust to the new auctioneer's speed and banter. And though I mistakenly bid against myself at least three times that afternoon, I did come home with a terrific old quilt and the excitement that comes from knowing that I now owned a piece of local history.

That locally made quilt and other auction acquisitions take on a new life when they become part of Breakfast Creek. Each comes with a story because it was part of some family's history. The walnut bed and matching chest of drawers in our guest room lived for over fifty years in a farmhouse near Mexico, Missouri. My canning jars go back to a time when Dr. John Parker's mother made jams and canned vegetables for their winter pantry. Each rug and chair and piece of pottery adds something of its past history to the history Kit and I are building at Breakfast Creek. When I bought a pressure cooker recently at auction, I was amazed to find that it came with its original box and a 1945 book of instructions. It was as though the owner knew that someday she would repackage it for a new owner and she wanted it to look as good as new.

Over time, I have learned that auctions are a time for visiting, bumping into friends, warming your hands around a hot cup of coffee, and revisiting the life of someone who has been a part of the community's history. Henry Klemme, the oldest citizen in Hartsburg, a small river town, seemed to have been a favorite in the community forever. When I learned there was to be an auction at Henry's farm, my initial reaction was one of sadness and loss. It was a bitterly cold day, but Henry's friends and family couldn't stay away. Long-time friends from Peace Church filled the kitchen with pies, chili and hot coffee while others visited around the yard. At one point in the bidding, the auctioneer held up what appeared to be an old axe. Suddenly, there was Henry, chopping firewood with those big, old hands. At that moment, I couldn't imagine anything around the yard being more valuable than that axe. It wasn't until I outlasted the one other bidder that I realized the axe was wooden—handle and blade alike.

Henry, I later learned, had been a member of the Woodmen of America. Perhaps that is what the axe symbolized. Or maybe it was a toy Henry made years earlier for one of his children or grandchildren. It doesn't really matter. I'm reminded of Henry and his life as a Missouri farmer and woodman each time I look at that wooden axe hanging on the mantel above our fireplace and I grow ever more certain that it has a story that perhaps someone will tell me someday. What I know is that everyone who left the Klemme auction that day with a piece of furniture or a dish or stack of bedding took a piece of the story that was Henry's life.

By our presence at that event, we each played a role in an age-old balancing act that enables life to go on. Through that act of passing one's things on to new hands and homes, we are all enriched. The auction becomes a celebration of life where the old becomes new again. Threads connect those in the community with others who have who come to remember their friend. Balance is maintained, and we are able to move forward, strengthened by what we have gained from friendship and sharing. (1994)

The Girls

Five kittens were born in the barn at Breakfast Creek this summer. Blanche and Scooter Boots had their litters in the same barn stall and shared the responsibility of raising them. After three months without names, I decided to call the two female kittens Sesame and Lilies.

Barn cats learn independence early on, and maintain a wild side in their world of hay bales and log piles. The tom kittens born this summer were the first to warm up to my sweet talk and allow me to brush them. Not so with Sesame and Lilies. Girl kittens are born believing the Italian proverb—"Girls and glass are always in danger." To them, I am still a giant danger on two legs every time I enter the barn.

"Sesame and Lilies" is the title of a lecture given by critic and writer John Ruskin in 1865. It is also the name of a French Restaurant on Sunset Boulevard that I frequented in an earlier decade of my life. The food was quite unusual—French cuisine blended with flavors of Southeast Asia. But mostly, I went there because the name was so fascinating.

It has been years since I've thought of that restaurant and its beautiful name. I wonder where the mind stores such curious bits of information? How is it that after ten years, when I am a distance of two thousand miles from Los Angeles and a century or more distant from the writings of John Ruskin, that the names Sesame and Lilies resurface as I stand in my barn pondering names for two kittens?

Here at Breakfast Creek, most of the animals are assigned names early on, but we often lump them together collectively in conversations. For instance, our gray house cats are referred to as "the girls." When the geese are grazing and behaving themselves, we might call to them as a group. "Hey, girls," Kit will say (even though he knows that half of them are ganders). The expression seems just as appropriate for the geese as it does for the cats. It is a term of endearment, a way of letting them know that they are part of the family.

My sisters and I were "the girls" in my childhood. We were constant companions as the family moved from one assignment to the next throughout my father's thirty-year career as an Air Force officer. Over the years, we shared rooms, took great pleasure in trying to scare each other silly after the lights had been turned out, sang musical scores while we did kitchen chores together, shared clothes, and now share visits as often as we can. We were, and hopefully will remain, the best of friends.

To my parents, my sisters and I still are "the girls," even though one of us has passed the half-century mark and I am fast approaching it. To a child, fifty seems ancient. To a parent, a child is a child is a child—whether their children are two or fifty. The child never catches up in age to the parent. Mom and Dad were twenty-seven years older than me as a child; and no matter how fast I tried to grow up over the years, they still are that much older than me today. That is the way it works in life.

Women define themselves and are described as "the girls" all through life. The definition fits whether the girl is five or fifty, because she is still her parents' child—their rascal daughter, their freckle-faced girl, the one with the scars on her knees from second grade roller-skating falls. And when she starts talking about rollerblading just this side of fifty, they know she is still that same little girl at heart.

When my grandmother was in her early eighties, I visited her in San Antonio. Granny had three women friends—Marie Holman, Betty Harris and Eileen Bockhoven—with whom she went out to dinner regularly. When a daughter or grandchild was in town visiting one of these ladies, the other women would host a little cocktail party. After an hour or so of storytelling and a Bourbon cocktail measured two-fingers strong, we would all pile into Granny's lime green Cadillac (the last year of the big fins) and very cautiously negotiate our way to a nearby restaurant.

During one of those evenings with Granny's circle of women friends, I sat back and let myself become a fly on the wall. The conversation wandered back to a time when their bodies were still as healthy and young as their minds were that night. No broken hips, no high blood pressure worries, no arthritis to make getting around a nuisance, no memory failures when stories were being recounted.

Their conversation lived in their youth. They were girls again, telling stories about their handsome husbands as U.S. Cavalry officers serving under General "Blackjack" Pershing and chasing Poncho Villa back into Mexico in 1917. I understood then that bodies and minds age differently. These four women always found a time and place in their conversations where they could be "girls" again, even if they did have daughters in their sixties calling them "Mom" and granddaughters forty years their junior calling them "Granny."

Last week, I was invited to a very special surprise birthday party. It was Nona Nistendirk's 90th birthday and she was sweet 16 again. Two longtime girl friends, Erna Beckmeyer and Martha Hesse, decided to drive up the formidable gravel road to Nona's hilltop home above the Hartsburg Bottoms and surprise her surprise her with two other visitors. It was very nice being included in that particular circle of women. Four decades separate Nona's age and mine, but that afternoon, we were all just friends, all just girls.

We passed around the stack of birthday cards Nona had received, and Erna shared news about the Peace Church quilting Circle. Plans were made for Erna and Martha to quilt together the next day and for Erna to take Nona to the Circle's monthly quilting meeting that Thursday. Nona was a charter member of the Circle, back when it was known as the Dorcas Society. Just think of the quilts she and these women have pieced together and the stories they have shared over all those years!

We celebrated the birthday girl in style. Nona insisted on bringing out a beautiful white tablecloth, even though the birthday menu was blueberry cobbler à la mode. After all, it isn't every day that "the girls" can drop in to visit over an afternoon cup of coffee.

I had my camera along and suggested that we go out into the yard for a picture of the birthday group before leaving. Dishes were washed, and there was a discussion of how awful everyone always looked in pictures. But, eventually the group headed in the direction of Nona's zinnia bed. Erna, Nona, and Barbara Beckmeyer were in the front and I stood behind them as we waited for Martha to walk over from the house.

"Over here, Shorty," Nona called out. "Come stand by me."

At that moment, Martha and Nona were "the girls" again, just as the Circle's quilters are when they meet each month; just as Granny and her friends were when they got together; and just as my sisters and I still are to my parents. Friendships and shared experiences connect women over a lifetime. That is the magic of a circle. And that is the beauty of being one of "the girls." (1994)

Nicolás

Touching the face of Nicolás, my fingers traced the rich colors of Spain. His is a face filled with light. Mediterranean light that comes in early June and stays late into each evening, turning all that it touches a rosy gold. Reflecting the color of the sun-bleached bricks of Iglesia de San Nicolas, the cathedral of his patron saint, built in Madrid in 1547. The cathedral in which he was baptized during our recent trip to Spain.

Saint Nicholas who lived in the A.D. 300s continues to be a popular saint of the Christian church today. He is patron saint of sailors, travelers, bakers, merchants, and little children. It is the perfect name for this beautiful child—the grandson of a family of bakers in Madrid and geographers from Missouri who love traveling back country roads and sailing to distant corners of the globe.

Nicolás at the age of 11 months is the spitting image of his paternal grandfather. Years ago, Kit's own father photographed Kit at close range, capturing forever the image of a baby boy with his head thrown back, engaged in a joyous explosion of laughter. Five decades and a few years later, that same bright spirit is alive in the darling little person Kit and I came to know during our week in Madrid.

As we had done on a prior trip, we stayed at the Hotel Santander, a small, family-run hotel on Calle Echegary in the heart of old Madrid. Lillian, the day clerk, was just as we had last seen her 18 months earlier. Smoking continuously and bantering in rapid fire Spanish with whoever passed her small check-in counter near the hotel's closet-sized lift. On the landing, an aged German shepherd—the hotel's security system—was sleeping exactly where we remembered him, strategically blocking anyone trying to ascend or descend the stairs.

After dropping off our luggage (minus one missing bag), we walked with Hayden, his wife Ana, and Nicolás to the Plaza Santa Ana for a *zuma de naranja* (freshly squeezed orange juice), *pan* (a sweet roll), and our first Spanish *café con leche* (coffee with steamed milk). The small plaza is quiet in the early morning hours with only an occasional stroller walking a dog in the park that forms the square's center. While I enjoyed my coffee, Kit carried his grandson out to the sidewalk for the first of many walks they would take together. At 11 months, Nicolás has discovered that shoes are made for walking, and these days he has little else on his mind.

Most evenings, the threesome would meet us at our hotel around 9:30 p.m. and we would stroll through the old neighborhood to one of the many small restaurants and cafes that can be found on every block. Madrid comes alive, we have learned, just about the time Midwesterners think about turning in for the night. So there we would be at 11:00 p.m. each evening, eating *tapas* (Spanish appetizers) such as *seta salteadas* (sautéed mushrooms with parsley and garlic), *pollo con patatas pobres* (chicken with fried potatoes), and *chuletas aliñadas con alioli* (lamb chops with garlic), and sipping *sangria* in densely packed, smoke-filled eateries with our son and his beautiful Spanish family. Being a baker's grandson, Nicolás was happy throughout the meal gnawing with his five baby teeth on a piece of hard bread and taking periodic walks with one or the other of his American grandparents.

My time alone with Nicolás came late one afternoon when Kit accompanied Ana to a bullfight. Knowing there was no way I could watch the unmerciful slaughter that Hemingway so graphically described in *Death in the Afternoon*, I offered to sit with my grandson and urged Ana to take my ticket. That way she could translate the ceremony of the bullfight for Kit and introduce him to her father, Marcos, who can be found every afternoon of the month-long season at the Plaza de Toros. Six dead toros and four hours later, Nicolás and I were fast friends and Kit had banished bullfighting from his wish list of things to see and do in *España*.

On Sunday evening, we gathered with the Martin family (pronounced Marteen), relatives, and friends at Iglesia de San Nicolás for the baptism of our grandson. He was dressed from head to toe in a blue the color of a Spanish sky in early summer. His godfather, Jose Luis Gahona Fraga, and his godmother and aunt, Marta Martin, stood with Hayden, Ana, and the baby during the ceremony and promised the Roman Catholic priest that they would help raise Nicolás in the faith into which he was baptized that evening.

A party followed the ceremony at the home of Azucena and Marcos, the maternal grandparents. Wine flowed, hors d'oeuvres and sweets were passed, and Kit raised toasts to the newly baptized child we had all gathered to celebrate that evening.

All too soon, it was time to begin our long journey home. We are now reliving the trip to Madrid through pictures and slides and look forward to the day that Nicolás makes his first visit to Breakfast Creek—a peaceful world where ducks and cats wander at will and nary a creature has ever had to face the red cape of a matador. (1997)

Chapter Seven

Cities

City Images and the Power of Pruning

The Walls of the City Speak

Celebrating Chicago

This Thing Called California

Dos Viajaros

Ah, Paris!

Outrageous Beauty

City Images and the Power of Pruning

This weekend, spring teased the Midwest, making it impossible to stay indoors. The vegetable garden was too wet to till, so I did not plant peas as one friend does each year on Presidents' Day. Warm days have brought early robins, as well as pesky flies and mosquitoes, and bluebirds and purple martins are scheduled to arrive at any moment. The urge to dig in the soil and get peas and sweet peas in before the March snows that surely will fall on us in the coming weeks eventually led me to the blackberry bushes along the east side of our pond. I could at least warm my back pruning dead berry canes and sculpting pathways between thorny bushes to make berry picking in late July less painful.

While our chunky dog sunned herself and the barn cats raced through the rabbit labyrinths that arching canes create, I bloodied by hands and forearms while ever so carefully shaping the summer berry harvest. It is work you cannot race through. Every step of the way, thorns grab at your pants and sleeves, and puncture your gloves. I thought of Sally Fields picking cotton in the film, *Places in the Heart,* her fingers wrapped in bloodied rags. Pruning and berry picking is hellish work, but the rewards are delicious.

That task should have calmed the eager gardener in me, but a sunny Saturday was followed by an even sunnier Sunday. When a friend offered me a truckload of horse manure mixed with sawdust aged to the texture of fine, shredded tobacco, my afternoon once again turned to my garden. To the asparagus patch, assorted flowerbeds, the herb garden and the strawberry patch. Shoveling and spreading horse manure, unlike berry pruning, is a painless exercise that leaves you free to wander around the yard with your thoughts. Mine, oddly enough, turned to New York City, where Kit and I spent the last week of February as urban explorers.

We did not expect to like New York City. After all, it was late February and one of the snowiest winters NYC has ever faced. Why had we planned to scout a July field trip for 50 geography teachers in the dead of winter, right in the middle of the Winter Olympics figure-skating competition? We knew New York City only casually, but enough to feel that we had bitten off more of the Big Apple than we were prepared to chew. After a flight delay in St. Louis, a long wait for baggage after arriving at LaGuardia Airport, and annoying problems getting an unoccupied room at the hotel, we were certain that the trip was a huge mistake. When we finally did get settled into our room that first night, we found ourselves carrying some mental baggage about big cities that was heavy indeed. Why, then, had we agreed to go to New York City in the first place?

Cities, like people, have personalities. Some we love; some we love to hate. We describe them as apples and oranges and accuse them of being filled with fruits and nuts. From a quiet base in the Heartland, it is easy to think of them as heartless places with no soul. At first glance, they can seem unmanageable, unfriendly, unwelcoming places. They fill huge spaces with monumental structures, creating vertical urban canyons—architectural reflections of the magnetism and energy that have drawn people to cities for thousands of years. You may not love cities, but you cannot help but be moved by their energy.

And moved we were. After a short, but solid night's sleep and a tasty, but overpriced breakfast, we hit the streets of the city. Maps in hand, we wove our way from 63rd Street at Lexington, east of Central Park, to Battery Park at the very southern tip of Lower Manhattan. We never ate another meal at the hotel after that walk and we rarely depended on a cab to get us where we were going. The city became our guide, and we came to realize that the key to knowing a city is walking through its neighborhoods. Taken as a whole, cities are overwhelming. Approached as a collection of neighborhoods—each with its own history and character—cities become more understandable and human.

The Staten Island Ferry provided a view of Lower Manhattan as 19th and early 20th century immigrants first saw the city, past Ellis Island and the Statue of Liberty. A walk through the lower East Side was a trip through streets that have been transient home to numerous immigrant groups on their way to other parts of the city or country. Streets like Hester, Delancy, Mulberry, and Mott—once the neighborhood of European Jews and Italians—are now part of a bustling Chinese region of the city. The Little Italy of New York today is an historic district, though you find few Italians living there anymore. Cities are fluid places, with immigrants of the 1990s replacing those of earlier migrations.

The complexion of the city changes profoundly as you explore it from north to south, and from east to west. Neighborhoods are also characterized by the economic activities that define them. Soho is a region of trendy art galleries and restaurants, Broadway at 36th Street the Garment District, and Broadway at 47th the Diamond District where Hassidic Jewish merchants can be seen conducting business only blocks from ice skaters at Rockefeller Plaza. Live theater is clustered around the Theater District farther up Broadway, and Central Park—an 840 acre lung in the heart of Manhattan—is home to museums, art galleries, a zoo, and skating rink.

Harlem provided us with our greatest challenge. It is its own island within an island. Taxis avoid it and are noticeably absent from its center at 125th Street and

Lenox Avenue (now Malcolm X Boulevard). We took a Sunday morning subway to 125th Street and Lexington with plans to walk the four long blocks west to Lenox. After three days of unchallenged urban exploration, our spirits were high. We were ready to embrace the center of the Harlem Renaissance of the 1920s when a caution flag was raised by a white policeman who I am certain must have thought we were hayseeds right off the farm. We were strongly advised by two policemen to take a bus those four blocks. As we emerged from the subway and stepped into Harlem at 8:30 a.m. on that Sunday morning, we were struck by how white we looked on those empty streets and—reluctantly—got on a bus like the rest of the folks. It was a strong lesson, and we are still trying to figure out how to bring 50 teachers to Harlem next July to explore its present as well as its past with some degree of comfort.

Before leaving the city, we visited an exhibit at the Museum of Modern Art to see a collection of Frank Lloyd Wright's drawings and models of some of the unique buildings the architect designed in the course of his amazingly long career. Cities for Frank Lloyd Wright were places to be avoided, and this retrospective provided us with an opportunity to review our own feelings about New York as we prepared to return to the Midwest. Like Frank Lloyd Wright, our hearts had remained in the Midwest; but, unlike him, we left the city knowing that we wanted to return to it and continue our exploration of its diverse neighborhoods.

Maybe dealing with cities is like pruning a blackberry patch. If you don't take the time to clear a path through the thicket, it remains an impossible tangle—a barrier keeping you at arm's length from the rich fruit visible within a dense thicket growing at the edges of a sunny, open meadow. Cutting through that maze will make future explorations fruitful indeed. (1994)

The Walls of the City Speak

There is much that can be learned from listening to the walls of a city. Cities are a collection of walls—some ancient, some modern. Walls are built to keep some elements out and others in, to isolate as well as insulate. Walls create lines that are vertical and horizontal, visible and invisible. They become borders for some and barriers to others, evolving along lines that are economic, political, racial, and religious. Sometimes friendly and loud, sometimes hostile and silent, the walls of the city speak volumes about times past and tell us much about the city today.

Kit and I returned to New York City last week to continue an exploration of its neighborhoods and districts begun a year ago. Coming into the city late in the afternoon, we experienced our first series of walls. A wall of pedestrian humanity vied with a flotilla of yellow cabs in an attempt to push through the narrow spaces that separate the city's high canyon walls. Our Haitian cab driver moved aggressively through a rough and rolling sea of pedestrians, cars, roller bladders, bicyclists, delivery trucks, sanitation vehicles, ambulances, NYPD blue and white vehicles, dogs being walked on short leashes, and tourists trying to figure out how to translate "Walk, Don't Walk" each time they attempted to negotiate a street crossing.

The cab's radio was tuned to a local classical music station as it moved through a sea of Manhattan humanity, following the flow around the southern end of Central Park to the Mayflower Hotel at 15 Central Park West.

The following morning, we took a red Downtown Express train from Columbus Circle, where streets are laid out in a predictable flat grid, to Rector Street, our exit point to Wall Street. This lower end of Manhattan is the city's first area of settlement and a maze of streets where canals once flowed. The old wall of Wall Street was an anti-British oak fence put up by Peter Stuyvesant, the Dutch governor, in 1653. The flimsy palisades of *Nieuw Amsterdam*, however, were never very effective as a walled fortification. Today the vertical walls of Wall Street are more formidable. In this world of high stakes financial trading where fortunes can be won and lost in the course of a day—or in a minute—solid walls provide a sense of security for those doing battle.

From Wall Street, we walked east to the Fulton Fish Market on the New York harbor. The ideal time to come to the fish market is before dawn when crates of fish are unloaded at the market's two huge warehouses. We arrived after buyers from the city's restaurants and markets had picked through the mountains of fish on ice, leaving only the smell and remainders of the morning's catch behind. No wall has ever been created that can hide the smell of fish.

Lunchtime found us at Cafe 121 on Mulberry Street in Little Italy. Here, the walls speak with painted scenes from southern Italy. Lucille, the co-owner and head waitress, calls everyone "Doll." Only the cafe's large gray cat, "Baby," rated a name of its own. When I stopped to sweet-talk Baby, I found myself next to a wall of framed pictures and letters. An envelope addressed to Mr. Dominick De Lucia, 108 Mulberry Street had "The White House" as the return address. Nearby was a framed letter dated Oct. 28, 1977 from Roselyn and Jimmy Carter.

Had Dominick De Lucia owned the restaurant? Had he reached the age of 100? "Almost," said Lucille, married to Dominick's grandson. On the same wall, a certificate told more of the story.

Ellis Island 1892–1992
Statue of Liberty-Ellis Island Foundation
Official Certificate of Registration
in the American Immigrant Wall of Honor
Officially Certifies that Domenico De Lucia, who came to America from Italy, is among those courageous men and women who came to this country in search of personal freedom, economic opportunity and future hope for their family. (Signed, Lee A. Iacocca)

There were also pictures on Lucille's wall of the 1961 New York Yankees World Champion baseball team and signed pictures of Mickey Mantle and Joe DiMaggio. A radio was tuned to an all '50s station. We ate our pizza listening to Peggy Lee sing "When in Rome, Do What the Romans Do," and Mel Torme reminded us that some things are "Easy to Remember, But So Hard Hard To Forget." The walls of Cafe 121 held glimpses into an Italian family that has been a part of this neighborhood for more than a century.

Later on, at 90 Orchard Street, we found ourselves in the heart of the Lower East Side tenements, the notoriously overcrowded and disease-ridden row house apartment buildings that were the first glimpse of life in America for European immigrants arriving in NYC between 1863–1935.

For more than an hour, we moved cautiously through dark, airless corridors and the rooms of two immigrant apartments recently reopened by the Hester Street Tenement Museum. One had been occupied by a family who came to America in 1870 from Germany; the other had been home to an Italian family who arrived in NYC in 1928. It is estimated that in the 70 years that the building was occupied, more than 10,000 immigrants lived in the cramped, dark quarters of 90 Orchard Street.

The five-story building had 6 privies in the alley behind the building and no electricity or heat. Apartments consisted of three small rooms—two 8'x 8' rooms connected by a 12'x 12' room used as a combination living room/kitchen. Only one room in each apartment had a window. To help pay the family's expenses, tenants often sublet their windowed room to boarders because it brought a higher rent. It was, therefore, not uncommon to have 10–12 people living in these tiny spaces. When we stepped outside in a light rain an hour later, it was like coming out of a dark, airless cave. We gulped in air and walked in the rain, our heads filled with what the walls of Adolpho and Rose Baldizzi's apartment had whispered of their life between 1928–35.

Our final day in the city took us to the north end of Manhattan where two neighborhoods as different as day and night exist side by side—one a predominantly white island of grand cathedrals and architectural richness located on the island's highest point; the other a sprawling, chaotic island of black poverty. These are the dissimilar worlds of Morningside Heights and Central Harlem, divided physically by a topography that has the world of the "Haves" looking out from heights created by a natural stone rock face at the flat, low-lying world of the "Have Nots"—the island of Black Harlem.

Nowhere in the city is the line between rich and poor, black and white, and one's sense of safety and danger as clearly defined by such an abrupt change in topography. A single rock wall separates these two worlds and creates a divide as deep as the Grand Canyon. Here the wall separates tongues of privileged English from those speaking Black English. Though the base language is more or less the same, inhabitants of these two worlds rarely communicate with one another.

For someone trying to understand a city, the trick is to go to the wall's edge and figure out how to get around its cultural divide. Venture into new territory and talk to people. Not only will you find that you speak the same language after all, you might get lucky as we did in Harlem and discover a place like Well's Soul Food Restaurant where fried chicken with a side of waffles and maple syrup is served with cornbread muffins and strawberry butter every Saturday from 10 a.m. to 3 p.m.

New York is a city with a world of stories. When you walk its streets, keep your eyes and ears open. Remember: The walls of the city speak. (1995)

Celebrating Chicago

Chicagoans love their city. It sits like an architectural jewel at the end of thousands of square miles of patchwork farm fields that stretch from southern Illinois to Lake Michigan. Born as a city in 1837, and architecturally reborn following the great fire of 1871, Chicago has been the Emerald City for many, their escape from whatever Kansas they left behind.

Since my first flight into and out of O'Hare International Airport over thirty years ago, I have weighed each opportunity to visit Chicago against the hassle of flying into O'Hare, until recently, the world's busiest airport. Only 55 minutes by air from St. Louis, O'Hare can seem worlds away from downtown Chicago, a distance costly in terms of cab time, dollars, and aggravation. A constant stream of traffic pours in and out of the city from every direction and the construction and reconstruction of the network of highways and expressways that link this great midwestern city to the nation is never-ending. Until recently O'Hare was the hub I merely passed through on my way to somewhere else. Chicago remained out of easy reach and out of mind.

This weekend, Kit and I flew to Chicago with two friends. Our agenda was simple—to explore the city and celebrate a birthday. Over our three days there, I overcame the psychic distance that has for too long kept me at the outskirts of knowing Chicago and I came away celebrating this American gem of a city. What a singular jewel it is in the crown of the Great Lakes nested atop the Heartland!

We found Chicago a friendly, breezy, spirited city of neighborhoods and immigrant energy, eager to please and ready to welcome the tens of thousands of visitors drawn to Chicago every season of the year. Our hotel housekeeper was a young recent import from Eastern Europe; cab drivers were an international hodgepodge that included a spirited Moroccan, a silent West African, an industrious Mexican, and one transplanted Clevelander who twenty years ago adopted Chicago as home. The cabbies had all come from different points of origin, but they were linked by two things—a heavy foot on the gas pedal and a sense of tremendous pride in talking about their city.

In reality, Chicago is many cities and worlds of neighborhoods. Saturday morning, we joined the mix of shoppers, tourists, and Chicagoans out walking or rollerblading in the unseasonably cool August temperatures blowing off the Lake and up Michigan Avenue. For shoppers, there are magnificent miles of opportunities to spend money that range from the Loop where you find the grand old department stores on State Street—Marshall Fields and Carson Pirie Scott—to the Gold Coast—chic Chicago at Oak Street—where names of shops ring of Paris, Rome and New York City.

An early morning walk south along Michigan Avenue's Magnificent Mile is the ideal way to see the city. The tree-lined sidewalks are wide and the skyline hypnotic, requiring repeated stops to look upward and admire the unique designs of the buildings along Chicago's downtown streets and avenues. It wasn't the stores that captured us, although they are dazzling in their display of style and color. It was the richness in architectural variety that Chicago, the city, so proudly expresses with pride.

A walk through Chicago's cityscape is an introduction to public art. Sunday afternoon, we spent several hours in the Chicago Art Institute visiting familiar works of some of our favorite artists, but found it too confining. After only two hours inside, we opted to experience Chicago's art *alfresco*, and headed back onto the city streets. Over 200 works of art have come to grace the parks and plazas of Chicago during the past century. The city itself is a living work of art. Among the architectural masterpieces of some of the greatest architects of the late 19th and 20th centuries, works of world renowned artists—Chagall, Calder, Moore, Picasso, and Miro—stand or hang in public spaces, accessible to the people of Chicago and visitors like the four of us who are willing to wander the city.

My favorite observation point in Chicago was not from the 103rd floor of the Sears Tower, although seeing a city from above is fascinating. The place where the city came together for me was at its point of origin, the site of Ft. Dearborn. At this spot, a grand pedestrian bridge commemorates the city's early history with statues and plaques, and the Chicago River flows back into the city from Lake Michigan. Across the bridge, the *Chicago Tribune* and *Chicago Sun-Times* keep a watchful eye over the comings and goings, wheelings and dealings of their city in all directions.

We stopped to read a quotation on the wall of the *Tribune* building—"Give me liberty to know, to utter and to argue freely according to my conscience, above all others" Milton—and to marvel at actual pieces of history built into the building's façade. Pieces of the Parthenon, the Alamo, the Great Wall of China, and the Great Pyramid, to name just a few, have been mortared into its foundation walls as if to say, "our word is as sound as these great monuments from times past. Herein lies the rock solid truth."

Our main agenda in coming to Chicago had been to explore the city, but it had also been to celebrate a birthday. Two years ago while on a business trip to Chicago, I discovered Trattoria Dinotto—a small, neighborhood Italian restaurant that I think is Chicago's best-kept culinary secret. Entering Dinotto's is like walking into a family-run trattoria in Italy. I have never finished a dining experience there in fewer than three hours, and have left each time wanting to tell lovers of truly wonderful Italian cuisine that this place is a delicious experience from the moment you enter its doors.

I had called ahead, certain its popularity and small size would require advance reservations.

"Christopher, four at 7 p.m. on Saturday the 6th," I said. "We'll be coming from Missouri."

When we arrived, Dino, the owner, was standing at the doorway and escorted us to the family table. He had remembered me, somehow, and I reminded him that I was, in fact, the lady from Missouri who loved his restaurant so much the two times I had dined there before that I wrote the editor of *Gourmet* magazine to sing its praises.

When Dino placed us in the hands of Andrea, the very same drop-dead handsome Italian waiter I have fallen in love with on my two prior visits, I knew the evening was going to be perfect. Wine was poured, toasts to Kit, the birthday celebrant, were raised, and portobello mushrooms and calamari were ordered. Then Dino reappeared with a thick black notebook filled with letters, opened up to the one I had written to *Gourmet*.

"Is this you?" he asked. *"C'est moi!"* I responded in my best high school French, hoping it would sound at least faintly Italian.

From that moment on, we were family. Second generation Chicago Italians, dining at Dinotto's designated family table. Parting, when the moment finally came, was like leaving home. We reluctantly stepped from the restaurant to flag a cab, and out the door flew Dino himself, right into the street to hail a cab for us. We parted with a hug of genuine friendship and taxied off to our hotel, all feeling that the birthday celebration had been a roaring success.

This week, I will write a second letter to *Gourmet* in my continuing effort to win recognition for my favorite little trattoria in Chicago. And each August hence, I will think back fondly on the city of Chicago and this particular birthday celebration shared with Kit and our two Missouri friends. (1994)

This Thing Called California

Years ago, the center of my world touched the shores of the Pacific Ocean. In those sun-filled days, the Heartland remained a distant state of mind. Today I am firmly anchored in the Midwest, and my oceans are fields of golden wheat and corn. Yet each time an opportunity arises for me to revisit Los Angeles, I eagerly return. For me, L.A. will always be a second home.

Preparing for a recent trip west, I looked through some slides for a presentation I was to make at UCLA. Years ago, Kit made a slide of a cover of a California magazine called *West*. I laughed as I looked at it and packed it along to share with my audience of L.A. geography teachers. It reads as follows: "What is this thing called California? It is a choice one makes, a blow one strikes for hope. No one ever wakes up one day and says, 'I must move to Missouri.' No one chooses to find happiness in Oklahoma or Connecticut...."

I looked at the date of the issue—February 1990. It must have been a really cold winter in Missouri that year. February can test even the strongest of us Heartlanders. February is when the snow fall is deepest, warm places seem most distant, and Midwestern kitchen pantries are well stocked with bags of California oranges and grapefruit because sunshine in liquid form is better than none at all.

Our recent return to Los Angeles came not in the depths of winter, but rather at the height of the Midwest's color-filled autumn season. I found it difficult to leave the brilliant silver maple at the entrance to Breakfast Creek knowing that any day a strong wind could blow through and strip it bare from tip to toe. So before leaving, I collected an assortment of maple leaves in brilliant fiery hues, baked four loaves of bread made from Hartsburg pumpkins, and packed along two terra cotta colored cow pumpkins that I'd bought from Strawberry Hills Nursery.

For us, driving in L.A. is a treat. We know how to merge into the steady flow of freeway traffic and if the going gets tough, we become savvy travelers on less traveled surface streets. To our delight, we still knew our way along the boulevards and downtown streets. Wilshire, Sunset, Pico, Olympic, Westwood and Beverly Glen Boulevard had all been part of my daily commute for more than a decade, along with the 405 and the Santa Monica Freeways. Like familiar friends, they were there to welcome us back for our brief stay.

Our final day in L.A. began early at the top of a side canyon in the Santa Monica Mountains where our friends, Don and Suzanne, live in an Italian modern home of their own design. Three years ago, Suzanne was making rosemary *foccacia bread* in her own kitchen and suddenly found herself baking hundreds and then thousands of loaves a week for local markets. Our friends now own *Buona Forchetta*, the hottest bakery in town. A food critic in *LA Weekly* described the phenomenon in the following way: "The demand for Suzanne's chewy, toothy, divinely Italian *foccacia*, *filoncini* and *bruschettine* grew so quickly that she had to acquire additional space, and her terrific 'hand-made breads' are now available in upscale markets all over town."

When we appeared in their still dark kitchen at 5 a.m. Don and Suzanne had already left for the bakery. On the counter, we found directions for operating the espresso machine, two glasses of freshly squeezed orange juice, an assortment of their bakery breads, and a note. "*Panettone* for toast, jams/marmalade in fridge, cereal in pantry. Have fun. Don't Work! Love, Suzanne."

At the bakery, neighborhood folks, movie stars, and celebrity chefs stop by early ..." according to the *Hollywood Reporter*. When we arrived there later that morning, Don was out making deliveries and Suzanne and her staff were busily taking orders for the following day. After sampling some of the day's breads, we were ready for a leisurely second breakfast *alfresco*. "You like Mexican food? Try Gloria's off Mississippi Avenue," Suzanne suggested. "You can sit outside and enjoy a platter of *burritos* or *huevos rancheros*."

As the morning commuters began filling the local streets with the hum of Monday back-to-work traffic, we enjoyed a leisurely read of the *LA Times* with our outdoor Mexican breakfast. We finished and then turned the car east onto Wilshire Boulevard and headed along its 10-mile course to its beginnings in the heart of the downtown.

When Kit and I moved from L.A. a decade ago, it had no subway. Now it is possible to take a subway downtown from Long Beach and into the city from areas of the San Fernando Valley. We parked at Union Station and entered an eerie world where real-life train commuters moved in and out of a make-believe scene being filmed by a local movie crew. Only in L.A., we thought.

Our exploration the rest of the morning was a sweet mix of seeing familiar landmarks and looking up at the towering growth that makes the new downtown feel like an urban canyon. Eventually, we made our way to a large open, five-acre parking lot on Temple Street. There, our son Hayden, an architect, will soon oversee the building of a monumental new Roman Catholic cathedral that will replace St. Vibiana's—L.A.'s oldest cathedral, that was badly damaged in the last earthquake.

Oh, City of Angels! What stories we will tell of you during the winter months in Missouri, as a $165 million cathedral begins to rise from deep in the ground in the heart of the City of Angels. Designed by Spanish architect Rafael Moneo, it is our son who will be on site to engineer its birth and completion. Oh, this thing called California! How we do love your dreams and outrageous energy! (1997)

Dos Viajaros

In Madrid's Atocha train station, a new sculpture sits quietly in the station's open interior space. A large suitcase, two pieces of hand luggage, an umbrella, and a man's hat have been bronzed as a tribute to those who have moved through this grand place over the past century. *El Viajaro,* (the Traveler), it is called.

Kit and I were among the travelers moving through Spain recently. *Dos Viajaros,* walking the streets and alleyways of Madrid's old quarter and exploring the Andalucian region of southern Spain. Spain had always before been a place that I knew through my studies of history and the arts. It was the guitar music of Segovia; the paintings of El Greco, Goya and Velazquez; Spanish olives and Valencia oranges; the legends of El Cid and Don Quixote; and *paella* (a Spanish rice and fish dish) and sherry from Jerez. Now, it was about to take on new images.

We had traveled to visit our son, Hayden—eager to learn the role played by Spain in the new European order of the 1990s. What we had not anticipated was the brilliance of Spanish light and its play on the landscapes of Madrid and the southern region of Andalucia. The same light that illuminated the canvases of Velazquez four centuries ago washed across every landscape we encountered in our week of travel through Spain.

Madrid was aglow in light that washed the façades of the city's old world buildings and carved wooden doors. Geraniums spilled from terra cotta pots over grillwork balconies. Blue and yellow tile street signs affixed to walls the color of sunlight directed us through the old quarter's rabbit warren of streets and plazas—Calle Alcalá, Plaza de la Villa, Puerta del Sol, Paseo del Prado—and back to our small family-run hotel on Calle Echegaray.

We followed our map loosely through Madrid's streets and neighborhoods in hopes of discovering the pulse of the city along the way. In the Plaza Mayor, local artists paint in the arcade that surrounds the plaza, once the heart of the city. In this ceremonial public square, heretics were burned alive during the dark period of the Spanish Inquisition. Bullfights occurred here into the late nineteenth century. It is a quiet place now. In the silence of the open square, it is easy to forget the passage of time and imagine the roar of the crowds that once gathered at this plaza's public spectacles.

The Prado, which houses the art collections of early Spanish rulers, attracts tourists from around the world and aspiring artists who copy the masterpieces of 15th and 16th century Spanish painters. But it was not this world-famous museum that pulled us in from Madrid's sunlight to walk among the masters. Having tired of the dark and tortured subjects at the heart of the Prado's often poorly lit galleries, we turned our attention to an extraordinary art collection that Spain acquired little more than a decade ago.

Housed in the Thyssen-Bornemiza Museum—the recently renovated Palacio Villahermosa—800 canvases from one of the world's finest private collections bring Renaissance through Twentieth Century masters together in a renovated space as beautifully conceived as the art itself. Rafael Moneo, the Madrid-based architect who converted the space from a palace to this exquisite public art gallery, is himself a student of Spanish history and a master of capturing light.

Moneo's use of earthen-colored walls and his ability to direct the play of light on each canvas left us eager to see the world of Moorish Spain that influenced this architect's design. His use of space and light became the subject of many late afternoon discussions over *café con leche* or a glass of *tinto* (red Spanish table wine), sometimes by ourselves, sometimes with Hayden, an architect in Moneo's Madrid office.

In Madrid, we experienced light. In southern Spain, we were bathed in it. There the sunlight along the Costa del Sol intensified the brilliance of the whitewashed houses and centuries-old churches built upon the rocky coastline between Salobrena and Malaga. It was in the warm region of Andalucia that the Moors built *alcazars* (fortified palaces) and left their strongest cultural imprint during the 700 years that they controlled Iberia.

After three days in Madrid, it was time for a road trip. With Hayden as our driver and guide, we set out in a rented Peugeot for Andalucia, with Granada and its famed Moorish palace of Alhambra as our first major goal. It was a day of driving through Spain's *Meseta,* a high dry plateau region of brown hills covered by mile after mile of olive groves and vineyards. At its southern reaches, this brown and often desolate-looking plateau runs up against the snow-capped Sierra Nevada Mountains that become the backdrop for the Alhambra, the Moors' last foothold in Spain.

The Moors understood how to capture cool air and light inside open spaces hidden behind fortified walls. They also gave local cooking an exotic quality by adding *seifran* (saffron), almonds, and peppers and introduced the art of adding sweets and pastries to Spanish cuisine. In Cordoba, another major center of Moorish culture in Spain, a 10th century gastronome named Ziryab introduced the Arab fashion of eating foods in a regular sequence, beginning with soup and ending with dessert.

It is impossible to talk about Spain without mentioning food and Spanish eating patterns. Flying from west to east, we arrived in Madrid at 7:30 in the morning and joined the rush hour jam of taxis, cars, and buses pouring into the central city. For local *Madrilenos* used to socializing until the wee hours of the morning, a cup of thick hot chocolate or espresso and *churros* (fried doughnut sticks for dunking) are the first fuel of the morning, eaten standing up at a bar or counter on the way to the office.

We soon learned that in Madrid, real breakfast *(desayuno)* doesn't happen until 10 or 11 a.m., and prompt service happens only if you stand at the bar while you eat. Most restaurants and *tapas* bars (serving small plates of hors d'oeuvres) don't open for lunch until 2 p.m. Meals go on for several hours and it seems that everyone smokes—before, during, and after meals. After work, groups of friends head for local *tapas* bars to socialize between 7–9 p.m. True *Madrilenos* rarely eat dinner until 10 or 11 p.m. Even still, there is time for a final round of the local *tapas* bars before sleeping a few hours and heading back to work the next morning

We will not miss the mealtime regimen of the Spaniards or the atmosphere of blue smoke that surrounded most meals, but we will miss Spanish *flan*—the heavenly caramelized egg custard that we ate as often as we could while in Spain. In his reflections on Spain in *Iberia,* James Michener wrote about a *bon vivant* he once met named Manolo Torres. Michener referred to him as *El gran flanero,* and described in great detail Torres' habit of making Spanish flan every day "as the angels make it." Sugar should be caramelized in custard molds over a fire. Eggs, sugar, lemon rind and milk are added and the molds are baked slowly by setting them in a water bath in a low oven. After an hour, the flan is refrigerated "until you have a guest arrive with a delicate palate."

Unmolded, flan is the color and flavor of Spain itself. It is the caramel brown of Spain's earth and the color of the walls in Moneo's Thyssen-Bornemiza Museum. The custard with its burnt crust recreates colors at the heart of Madrid and Andalucia. This light dessert of the angels is only one of many sweet memories that we have carried back to Breakfast Creek—*Dos Viajaros* exploring the layers of light and life that are the essence of Spain. (1994)

Ah, Paris!

It was a day much like today. Sunny. Crisp. Filled with the warm light of autumn that washes all that it touches in apricot and rosy plum. Traveling on the Eurostar high speed train from London, we crossed under the English Channel and arrived at the *Gare du Nord* train station in NE Paris three hours later. It was 2:00 p.m. on a Saturday afternoon. Time to drop my brief linguistic adaptation of British English and shift *rapidement* into my less than confident French.

Within seconds of wheeling our baggage past the security point and into the heart of this grand old train station, our party of four entered the radar screen of an unsmiling Algerian with a gray mustache. His loosely laced, tread-bare tennis shoes produced the shuffle of someone plodding through life without ever lifting his feet from the floor. "Taxi?" he asked flatly while attempting to take my luggage. "Money exchange," I replied, tightening the grip on my bags. "Follow me," he said, pointing with his dark eyes to a booth near the exit. As the four of us exchanged pounds and dollars for francs, our self-appointed middleman doggedly remained at a shadow's distance, determined that for organizing our first taxi in Paris, he alone would be handsomely rewarded.

And so it was that we four ended up stuffed into an Algerian driver's Parisian taxi—an impossibly small cab—given the bulk of our combined luggage. With the trunk loaded to capacity, three of our group squeezed into the back seat holding hand luggage and camera bags. Because I had organized our hotel reservations, I took the passenger seat up front. *Où allez-vous?* "Where to?" the driver asked. Opening my map book of Parisian neighborhoods, I directed him to *l'Hotel Grande Leveque, 29 rue Cler*. Appearing a bit miffed at the implied suggestion that he might not know the way to *rue Cler*, he dismissed the map with a wave of his hand and a curt, "But, of course."

Negotiating by cab from the city's northeast quadrant to our hotel near the Eiffel Tower in SE Paris is normally possible along one of the north-south boulevards leading to the Seine River. There any one of a number of bridges or tunnels takes you over to the *rive gauche* (Left Bank) and Paris' most famous landmark. But on this particular afternoon, it would take all of our driver's patience and driving skills aided by my Michelin plan (map) of Paris streets to complete our journey. Striking workers opposed to a 35-hour workweek had driven empty tour buses into the city, effectively blocking the major north-south traffic arteries. Inching his way around traffic stalled at each of these critical routes to the river, our driver bemoaned the chaotic situation created by such tactics and spoke passionately of the impossible conditions they created for taxi drivers trying to earn a livelihood.

Unable to turn south, our driver maintained a westward course, crossing every neighborhood between the train station and the Arc de Triomphe in NW Paris. Once there, we plunged head on into the great rotary speedway encircling the monumental arch, fed by 12 spoke-like avenues without benefit of traffic lights or lanes. *Très dramatique!* I said, stunned by the Arc de Triomphe's grandeur and the daring, roulette-style lane changes being undertaken by our fearless driver. "*Mais non,*" he replied, explaining that I had described the historic monument as "tragic." *Formidable?* I asked, hoping to correct my gaffe. "*Oui,*" he said approvingly. "*C'est formidable.*"

By now, our driver had warmed to his new role as tour guide. Turning onto the *Pont de l'Alma* bridge, he pointed to a gilded sculpture of a flame near the entrance to the tunnel under the Seine. "It is where Princess Diana died," he says, pointing out the flowers and messages left by those who come to the spot each day. "*Dramatique?*" I asked. "*Oui,*" he nodded. "*Très dramatique.*"

With the river behind us and the Eiffel Tower on the horizon, I put away my maps and pointed to the street ahead. "*Allez a droite.*" "Go right," I said. "Stop where *rue Cler* becomes a pedestrian market street." Soon, we were eagerly unloading luggage and saying *au revoir* to our driver. Standing at the curb, we could not believe our good fortune. Before us for as far as we could see were picturesque shops, market stalls, outdoor cafés, and a yellow sign that read, *Hotel Grande Leveque.*

After checking in, Kit and I took the hotel's phone booth-sized lift up to room 53, advertised as having a view of the Eiffel Tower. Standing together on our balcony five floors above *rue Cler*, I sighed, unable to take my eyes from the scene before me. Ah, Paris! *Magnifique!* Truly *formidable!* (1999)

Outrageous Beauty

January 26th was a sunny day aboard the *Royal Viking Sun*. At 9 a.m. in the South Pacific, it was only 2 p.m. on the prior day in Missouri. It would be another 19 hours before Hartsburg would greet the same morning, most likely wearing snow boots and winter trappings. My thoughts on that morning were not of snow, but rather of the ports we had visited over the past two days—the Bay of Islands and Auckland on New Zealand's North Island.

Like most islands within the Pacific's Ring of Fire, New Zealand is volcanic, with geothermal geysers that are tapped for energy. It is a country of spectacular natural beauty, with volcanoes and lakes on North Island and a line of continuous mountains down the western side of South Island, with glaciers in its Southern Alps.

Today, there are large pine plantations all over New Zealand, and farms where crops of wheat, oats, and barley are raised. It is the home of the fuzzy, green kiwi fruit, named after New Zealand's flightless national bird. But much earlier, sheep became the primary product when refrigeration made shipping trade with England possible in the 1880s. Today, there are 3.5 million people and 75 million sheep living in an area about the size of the British Isles. Most New Zealanders are descendants of 19th-century British settlers, and of Maori seafarers who arrived from Polynesia almost a thousand years ago. In their eyes, New Zealand is "God's own country," with all the geographical diversity of an entire continent.

The Bay of Islands on North Island was our destination as we followed the routes of earlier navigators. It had been an important area of early Polynesian settlement and the scene of contact with early European explorers, including Captain James Cook. Whalers and sealers followed and began trading with the Maori in Russell, a frontier town in the bay that became the center of trade in New Zealand in the early 1800s. Russell had once been a gold town with a rough reputation as "Hell Hole of the Pacific." Today, it is a quiet resort town reached by ferryboat where New Zealanders enjoy spending their summer vacation at one of the local hotels or anchored offshore in the harbor.

We arrived at Russell in the early afternoon and stopped for a lemonade and ice cream at the Duke of Marlborough Inn. From our outdoor table facing the Strand and narrow beach, we looked out on the bay filled with colorful sailboats and reflected on images of our first day in New Zealand. In a walk around Russell, we had stopped by a quaint old white-framed church. For some time, I had wandered through the cemetery that spread peacefully over the quiet church grounds, reading the town's history in the names recorded on the grave markers. I read of the seamen from Russell with English names, lost on the H.M.S. *Hazard* that sank in the defense of the town in 1845—

> "The warlike of the Isles, the men of field and wave.
> Are not the rocks their funeral piles,
> The seas and shore their grave...."

I also read a tribute to Tamari Waka Nene, chief of Ncapuni, the first of the Maori chiefs to welcome the Queen of England's sovereignty in New Zealand. "Sage in counsel, and renowned in war," his tall granite stone read, "he faithfully upheld the government of the colony for 31 years, and died in 1871, regretted by all the inhabitants of the island at Russell."

Earlier in the day, we had visited the Treaty House and Maori Meeting House in the historic area of Waitangi, immediately across the bay. There, the story of Maori culture and society is carved into the pillars and ridgepole of the thatched meetinghouse. Inside, the rafters represent the ribs of notable Maori ancestors; the interior is the chest of the ancestor.

After removing our shoes, we entered the thatched structure through a massive carved door and sat on the hardwood floor. A sound and light show told the story of the Treaty of Waitangi, signed by the Maori and the British in 1840. A single light projected from above moved up and down the intricately carved and patterned interior walls. In the dark, I imagined the walls as the tattooed faces and bodies of past Maori warriors. The light traced each carved tattoo, fierce and bold in design, meant to frighten foes while rewarding a warrior's bravery in battle.

"Outrageous beauty," I thought, as my eyes followed the wild designs.

As the light and voice moved over the story-filled walls, I slipped into another place and time. To rural Iowa in the early 1970s. To a farmhouse where I stopped once while exploring back country roads with my camera. To an old farmer who had been a sailor in his youth and learned the art of tattooing.

I was in my mid-20s, just back from exploring life as a teacher in Southeast Asia, eager to learn what was next in my life's plan. At that particular moment in time, I was drawn to that farmhouse for no reason I have ever been able to explain. On a thin piece of paper, I drew a design that looked like a cross between a Chinese character and the letter H. The design was then pressed against the skin below my left inner ankle and traced with an ink-filled needle to create the tattoo that has traveled with me now for almost twenty-five years.

If a tattoo is a record of one's life in the Maori tradition, mine was a record of what was to be. I would marry Kit, fluent in Mandarin Chinese, and travel with him to China and Hong Kong five times over the next 20 years. My stepchildren's names would be Hayden and Heidi. I would teach in Los Angeles and take an assignment in Washington, DC, then migrate to and fall in love with a rural farm town in the Heartland called Hartsburg.

Sitting in the Maori Meeting House, worlds away in distance and time from the rural farmhouse, I traveled back over the roads my life has followed since that day in Iowa. As I sat cross-legged on the floor, each highway and dirt road could be traced in the small "H" etched into my ankle. I rubbed the tattoo and smiled.

"Outrageous beauty," I thought to myself. "Think of the roads we have traveled together!"

To understand why and how something is recorded before it has happened, you must understand what the Aborigines of Australia refer to as "dreamtime." Only then can you understand the story of a tattoo that links a back country road in Iowa to a Maori meeting house in New Zealand, separated by half a world in space and a quarter of a century in time. But that is another story and we have miles to travel still before we are there. (1995)

Chapter Eight

Other Places

Tangerine

From a Distance

Hands at Work

A Wedding in Milan

Back of Beyond

Roads Taken

Tangerine

This Labor Day weekend, two friends invited us to float a stretch of Courtois Creek just east of Steelville, Missouri. A road trip was planned that would allow us to explore at a leisurely pace much of the first afternoon, wandering the hilly back roads of Maries and Gasconade counties, exploring and engaging in viticulture research when we found a winery along the way.

After winding over and down back county roads for several hours, we arrived at the Ferringo Vineyard near St. James late in the afternoon. From a picnic table overlooking the vineyard, we enjoyed a taste of Missouri's wine country along with a light picnic of cheeses and local sausage. The stop was a step back in time. A reminder of the fact that fine wines have been a part of Missouri's heritage since the mid-1800s, and of a time early in the 20th century when the state ranked second only to California in the nation in wine production.

Back on the road, we turned toward St. James and entered Crawford County. Highway 8 took us east into Steelville, past the Brown Shoe factory and a sign that reads, "1990–2000, Population Center of the United States." Then, a second sign reminded us of why we had come. "Steelville," the sign proudly boasted, "the floating capital of Missouri."

Names of nearby towns and rivers in the region connect this corner of the Ozarks with worlds and times that now lie oceans away. Bourbon, Courtois (pronounced *coat-away*) Creek, and the Bourbeuse River, are place names Ozarkified over the years in local speech, recognizable as French only when read on a map. From where we had begun at Breakfast Creek five hours earlier, Steelville seemed a world away in both distance and time.

There was a time when the world truly did come to Steelville. As long ago as the Roaring 20s, vacationers from St. Louis, Kansas City, and Chicago—nearly 400 miles away—were drawn during the hot summer months to dude ranches and fishing resorts tucked away in this beautiful region of the Ozark headwaters of the Meramec River.

On a previous road trip to Steelville four years earlier, Kit and I heard stories of a resort lodge with 56 guest rooms and truly grand common rooms that had opened in 1922, situated on a high bluff overlooking the Meramec River and green valleys of the Ozarks. Following directions we had been given by a local merchant, we found the old lodge nested in a residential neighborhood at the top of Grand Drive, high above the town center and rail line. Then, only a silent ghost of its past self, it had been closed up and guestless for going on a decade.

Kit and I mentioned the old lodge to our friends. They'd never heard of it but we all wondered if by chance someone had brought it back to life in the four years that had passed since our last exploration of the town. Unable to resist, we turned north off of Main Street from the center of town and nosed our car up the hill that begins its steep climb just beyond the railroad tracks. Amazingly, after only one wrong turn, we found Grand Drive again and followed it around until we reached the carriage drive at the entrance to the old lodge. A freshly painted sign read "Wildwood Springs Inn."

To our delight, lights were on inside the building and the driveway was filled with the cars of guests who were once again discovering this ghost of another era. Our friends were dumbfounded at the scale of the structure and the fact that in all of their trips to Steelville over the years, they had never heard anyone mention this old inn. And yet, when it opened on Memorial Day in 1922, 2,500 people came, and there was a parade through Main Street in town. Guests came by train from St. Louis 85 miles away, and carriages brought them up Grand Drive to the Wildwood Springs Inn.

There was no discussion needed about where we would have dinner that evening. We entered the spell of the Wildwood Springs Inn and took another step back in time. Time had stopped in the guest lobby somewhere back in the 1940s. Oak-framed couches and reading chairs spaced generously around a central hardwood floor had the same soft leather cushions guests had found irresistibly comfortable half a century earlier. Near the stone fireplace at the back of the open lobby, a flyer posted news of the evening's live entertainment—a dance band was playing music from the 1940s at 7:30 that evening.

As the four of us dined on a long screened porch overlooking the valley below the Inn, I suggested that we raise our glasses in a toast to peace. Fifty years ago to the day, the peace treaty ending World War II had been signed aboard the USS *Missouri*. Then I told them about a phone conversation I had had the prior morning with my father.

Dad had been re-reading *American Caesar,* William Manchester's biography of Douglas MacArthur, and had come across a description of the moment at 9:25 a.m., September 2, 1945, when MacArthur completed penning his name on the treaty that ended WWII in the Pacific and announced in a steely voice, "These proceedings are now closed." At that moment, Manchester wrote, the Japanese were led away. MacArthur put an arm around the shoulders of Admiral Halsey, on whose flagship the historic signing was taking place, and asked, "Bill, where the hell are those airplanes?" (referring to a flyover that the admiral had promised him).

The following line in the book triggered a distant memory my father had not spoken of in fifty years. Manchester described the moment in this way. "As if on signal, a cloud of planes—B-29s and navy fighters—roared across the sky from the south. They joined ... in a long sweeping majestic turn as they disappeared toward the mists hiding the sacred mountain of Fujiyama. In that instant, World War II ended."

Dad then began to fill in footnotes to this history that he had personally witnessed. An armada of 1200 B-29s and P-51s had flown from bases on Guam, Saipan, and Tinian and assembled in a massive V-formation over Tokyo. The formation was then joined by navy fighter planes. At the precise moment that MacArthur was scheduled to complete the signing of the treaty, the airplanes flew over the deck of the *Missouri,* turned in the direction of Fujiyama, and headed back to their bases in the Pacific.

"All but the lead B-29," Dad added. "It dropped down to 300 feet as the others headed south, and for the next 45 minutes *we* flew alone over the city of Tokyo, surveying the firebomb damage." William Earl Riggs—a 26-year old Captain in the United States Air Force with a wife named Alice, a two-year old daughter named Molly, and a second daughter who would be born the following month and be named Cathy Lynn—was the pilot who flew the lead B-29 in that amazing flying armada in a salute to General MacArthur in Tokyo Bay that historic morning fifty years ago. Bill Riggs ... my father.

As I finished telling the story, the band began to play in the front lobby. While our friends went on a tour of the building with the Inn's proud new owner, Kit and I walked out onto the dance floor. I knew the song. Remembered it from a recording by Helen O'Connell that Dad used to play when I was a little girl. *Tangerine ... my heart belongs to Tangerine.* The music took me back fifty years to a moment when, for a brief while the entire world stood quietly at peace. (1995)

From a Distance

From a distance, I see four geese walking on water. The pond is frozen and eerily still. The geese make a comic quartet in their silent procession toward the pile of grain that I threw on the ice at dawn this morning. Back inside, in the warmth of our kitchen, I look out the window and watch them eat. A cup of coffee and steamed milk warms my hands, and already I have forgotten the feeling of winter's bite.

From a distance the bank around the pond could be a snowy hillside in Bosnia. Winter seems to know that place well. Leaders have returned from peace talks in Dayton, Ohio, and once again there are new postures over how to partition the pieces of the former Yugoslavia left after four winters of uncivil war. In Dayton, peace was a hard battle of words wrestled onto paper. In Sarajevo, peace is a concept that has almost been forgotten.

From a distance, we watch the first American troops arrive in Tuzla to begin the task of giving this wretched place hope for a future. Bosnia will touch our lives differently now. We will finally feel the cold of their winter and understand the starkness of their lives as American troops come into the line of sniper fire in ethnically divided neighborhoods and tread on a broken infrastructure made even more treacherous by the presence of an estimated six million uncharted land mines.

I refill my coffee cup and steam another pitcher of milk. Our chunky black Lab is snoring on her pillow in the kitchen and the house cats have all decided that it is still too cold to venture out, even with the temptation of fat little birds at the feeders just beyond the pantry door. From a distance, another ten cats are hibernating in deep nests of straw inside the barn. Their coats have grown thick like rabbit fur. Unlike their softer house cat cousins, they have never felt the warmth of the kitchen floor vent that I am standing over. Like the geese, they have learned the trick of walking on water when the pond grows still and the ground is white with snow.

From a distance, I hear the voice of a friend in Los Angeles. We spoke this week and he has been in my thoughts ever since. We once trekked together in the mountains of Nepal. The photograph that I keep of him in my studio is one that I took twenty years ago. Our trip overlapped his sixtieth birthday, and we were traveling down the Irrawaddy River in Burma at a pace made glacial by the weight of the humanity crowded onto the boat's decks. From that place framed long ago by time and distance, the world was for a few moments a peaceful place.

From a distance, we could not see the cancer that has now invaded my friend's life. Sadly, I cannot bring back the moment of inner peace that I see on his face in the 1975 photograph. Now, in his daily battle to regain his former health, he views the world as an increasingly dark, inhumane, and ultimately hopeless mess.

We talked about Breakfast Creek and the world of Boone County that I write about in my weekly newspaper column. To my friend, the world that I am looking out on from my kitchen window is an unreal world. A landscape painted by an idealistic and perhaps naive artist. From a distance, he argues that the same cancers that already fill America's urban neighborhoods and make people mean-spirited are bound to come to Boone County as well.

I look at life differently, and sadly will never change my friend's read on the world. Our disagreements are not new. When I lived in Los Angeles and taught in one of the urban neighborhoods that now seem hopeless to him, that place took on a human face. It was no longer just a black, inner city neighborhood. The streets around the school had names that I recognized as the addresses of my students.

Over a thirteen-year period, I taught younger brothers and sisters of former students and came to know some of their parents. While I couldn't fix all of the social problems in the community or heal the accumulation of racial tensions that have been a part of L.A.'s story for too long, I did challenge my students to look at the world beyond their own neighborhood. Teachers rarely know if they have had a lasting impact on their students' lives. From a distance, I continue to hope and believe that I have.

A month ago, when Prime Minister Yitzak Rabin was assassinated, I recalled the impact that President Kennedy's death had on the American people 32 years ago. When President Kennedy was assassinated, I was an eighteen-year-old freshman at the University of Nebraska, on my way from lunch to a 1:00 p.m. history lecture. Five years later, I was brushing my teeth on the back porch of my house at Pranakorn Teachers College near Bangkok, Thailand, when a student bicycled up to the house with the news that Robert Kennedy had been shot.

From a distance, I still remember the concern of my Thai friends whose genuine sympathy helped when I felt isolated from events taking place on the other side of the world in my own country. In the week following Prime Minister Rabin's death, I pulled a faded yellow business card from an old address book and read a name that I had forgotten in the twenty-five years since it was given to me. On the card was the name "Aliza Ben-Artzi, advocate, Tel Aviv," with an office address and phone number.

We met in 1970 on a flight from New Delhi to Agra, enroute to visit the Taj Mahal. I had completed my Peace Corps assignment in Thailand and was just beginning a month-long solo trip back to the States with India as my first stop. I was fortunate that day to make the acquaintance of Mrs. Ben-Artzi, an Israeli attorney, and another woman from England whose name I no longer recall. They took me under their wings and invited me to share a car for the drive from the airport to the Taj Mahal.

That day was our only meeting, but it has remained in my memory all of these years. As I read Mrs. Ben-Artzi's address, I realized that I have lived at nine different addresses since returning to the States after completing my Peace Corps assignment. What, I wondered, were the chances of reaching my Israeli acquaintance at the address on that old business card? I decided that I would at least try.

From a distance, I wrote about how much our day together all those years ago had meant to me as I was traveling alone in an unfamiliar country. There was a little news of my life now, but most of the letter was to share the sadness that I felt, that most Americans felt, at receiving news of Prime Minister Rabin's assassination. I mailed the letter to the address on the old business card, hoping against the odds that it would reach my friend.

Several weeks later, an aerogramme arrived from Israel. Mrs. Ben-Artzi had received my letter, and recalled our day at the Taj Mahal. From a distance, she touched on the tragedy Israel is currently living through and then moved on to her retirement, her husband, and her three children. Her oldest grandson, she wrote, is now serving in the Israeli army.

Now, when I view events in Israel, the distance will no longer seem as great. I will consider events as they touch my friend and her family, and I will share with her my world at Breakfast Creek. In a friendship, distance and time should never matter. It might even help us see the world more clearly. As the English author John Fowles wrote in *The Magus*, "The most profound distances are never geographical." (1995)

Hands at Work

It is the middle of October and three hours remain before dawn. Wafting breezes have stirred up a dry rustling in the fallen walnut leaves at Breakfast Creek. The cat staring out a bank of windows in our upstairs bedroom watches for signs of mice dancing in the waning moonlight. Indian summer has made the night too warm for either a blanket or sleep. Three time zones to the west, a drifting, old native Alaskan waits out the 27° night in downtown Anchorage where a 24" snowfall has just buried the last traces of autumn. Suddenly, my feet are cold and I am on Fourth Avenue, a block from the Anchorage Hotel.

Seven days a week, Blondie's Cafe opens its door at 6:00 a.m. to all who have traveled to this distant frontier city. Just mornings ago, Kit and I were the first to arrive, our body clocks still on Midwestern time. Our minds, on the other hand, were keenly focused on the moment, and at that particular moment, on reindeer sausage and a short stack of sourdough pancakes. The aroma of freshly brewed coffee warmed the room, an eclectic mixture of 1950s rock and roll memorabilia and pure Alaskan Iditerod dog sled racing motifs. The old native Alaskan who entered after us takes the booth across from ours and orders a cup of coffee. Cindy, a spirited, black-haired waitress, waits for the rest of his order, sensing already that coffee is all that the man can hope to get.

Before the Anchorage McDonalds on the corner of Fourth and E closed less than a year ago, coffee was affordable. At Blondie's, coffee is $1.00 and the man has only 80¢ in the pocket of his Army-Navy Surplus jacket. Choosing compassion over cents, Cindy fills the man's cup generously and nests it directly in his stiff, brown hands. We all sigh in silent unison, knowing that it is the first warmth the old man has felt in many hours. Kit changes our order to eggs and a bowl of Blondie's original oatmeal. "Give the pancakes and sausage to the old gentleman," he tells Cindy when she circles by to refill our coffee cups. Then, as an afterthought, "Come to think of it, we're not as hungry as we thought we were."

Later that same day, at the Cook Inlet Bookstore, I picked up a card that reminded me again of the native Alaskan. The image on the card is of a man wearing a soiled canvas jacket and flannel shirt. His tired hands are resting on the heavy links of anchor chain that hang over one shoulder. Oil and grease delineate every line and crevasse on the sun-baked hands. The photographer entitled the photograph "Hands at Work." An Alaskan oil worker. A Midwestern corn farmer.

A Puget Sound fisherman pulling up anchor after a solitary night on the water. Rootless in the city, our native Alaskan's brown hands rest idly on the table against his cup of coffee. In another place located deep within the map of this man's heart, there is a warm, tribal place where his brown hands once hunted and fished, but that place must have seemed like a distant dream that cold morning.

In 1947, the 1,500-mile Alcan Highway (previously used as a military supply route) was opened to adventurous settlers eager to homestead the Alaska Territory, America's "Last Frontier." Then, with a lot of luck, spare auto parts, and a supply of spare tires, the overland journey took close to a month. Today, less than a day of travel time separates winter in the Alaskan north from late autumn in the Midwest. In terms of spatial distance, it is a journey from the mid-latitude Corn and Soybean Belt to a region just below the Arctic Circle, crossing sixty degrees of longitude. From Breakfast Creek, the journey is over 4,000 miles and takes the better part of a whole day spent in the air and in four different airless airports.

Sounds and icy glaciers, snowy coastal mountains and archipelagoes, straits and Whidbey Island—my artist friend Maxine's world—pass under our wings as we fly homeward, following the curve of the continent down to Seattle. There, we see urban densities again that seem more real than the frontier scale of downtown Anchorage.

Leaving Seattle behind, I looked down for the next three hours and fifty minutes at the West's vast and ever-changing map. It is a living landscape. Seattle and Washington look much like the Midwest from above, still green but colored increasingly with the oranges and golds of October. Neatly organized suburban developments and waterfront homes on the sound gradually flow into farmland stretching between forests and streams. Flying east toward the Cascades and Rocky Mountains, we gain altitude until the view below is only clouds. A lunch of ravioli is served at 36,000 feet somewhere over Montana. Amazing, I thought to myself, that not one of the 200 passengers or crew aboard our magic carpet has marveled aloud at the wonder of flight in this transit. Surely they would have sixty years ago in the age when Richard Halliburton kept his readers spellbound with stories of his daring and fantastical air flights to the world's most exotic corners.

In the silence of readers and sleepers that follows ravioli and coffee, I find that I cannot take my eyes from the living map that is passing beneath our wings. Montana emerges from the clouds as an ancient brown land, wrinkled and worn, pushed up and weathered flat again. Looking south, a line of transverse hills becomes a thundering herd of buffalo racing north across the broad spans of brown flatness, leaving a trail of white dust behind. Seen at ground level, the brutes are actually buttes. The dust is moist clouds pushing south over the relief on this otherwise flat stretch of dry land.

Farther east as we approach the Dakotas, center-pivot-irrigation systems create geometry of their own across the arid landscape. Rotating arms transforming marginal dry lands into farmland, inscribing giant crop circles, coloring the brown earth shades that range from winter wheat green to the yellows and golds of soybeans, milo and corn.

Crossing Montana, it occurred to me that had I fallen from the plane onto the map below, I would be absolutely alone. This, of course, is not the case, but from the air it appeared to be so. Finally, a suggestion of road appeared and I was reassured that the earth below was alive and settled. Lives here. Lives there. Distant, but connected by networks laid over and across the land.

As we passed over Mt. Rushmore near Rapid City, South Dakota, there was more order on the land. Straight lines. Rectangular fields of wheat showing bright green that look more the color of summer. More crop circles now. Brown, tan, green, textured, lined, circles within circles. Then, a pattern of rectangles, farm roads laid out in a perfect grid.

Finally, amidst the overall feeling of dryness that makes the lands of the American West so fragile, a river appeared. I wondered if this is where all the brown mud that came into Hartsburg in the Great Flood of '93 began its destructive journey. Could it possibly have come from such a dry place? It was a mean, drunken river when it came into town three summers ago. I sense from its wild, meandering tendencies that it is headstrong and narrow at this upper stage of its course. Unwilling still to conform to the rather flat and staid order on the land, the young river boldly ribbons, snakes, and winds any which way it pleases.

When Omaha is called to our attention by the pilot, the Missouri River has become a mature band of green coursing with a sense of purpose across the flat farmscape. I point out a textbook perfect oxbow to Kit—a final attempt by the mighty river to wander before it straightens out and speeds on its collision course with the Mississippi River at St. Louis.

Floating above Earth in our encapsulated microclimate, we have traveled from a frozen dawn in Anchorage to twilight and balmy 76° temperatures in southern Boone County. Fed and watered, we are carried eastward on the Jet Stream as if on a magic carpet. It has been a day filled with thoughts of aging brown hands, their lines the map of an old Alaska native's personal journeys and the stories of other hands that have changed the face the American West. Hands at work.

It is now late in the morning, and my writing for the day is done. My hands come together, opening outward. I read again the journey that connects me to the old native, and reach out to touch his brown hands across the miles. (1996)

❖ ❖ ❖

A Wedding in Milan

The road from Breakfast Creek to Milan, Italy, is a story with many layers. Like the city of Milan itself, the story is rich in color and character, history and international flavor. At times it is an impossible maze of narrow, winding paths that ultimately spill into a grand *piazza* facing a cathedral. At one level, it is the love story of Cinzia Maria Corio of Concorezzo (Milan) and Mark Anthony Holman of Compton (Los Angeles). At another level, it is the story of a long time friendship that has grown over the past 14 years between a young man and his teacher. It is also the story of an extended family in Italy and the marriage of their only daughter to that same young man four years after the two met in Moscow.

Over the past four years, news of the growing romance of *Marco e Cinzia* reached Breakfast Creek from distant places—from Boston where Mark graduated from Harvard University, from Russia where they met while studying at the Pushkin Institute in Moscow, from Los Angeles where Mark grew up and still has family, from Concorezzo in Italy where Cinzia's family has deep roots, and from Portland, Oregon where Mark and Cinzia will soon establish roots of their own.

I feel fortunate to have had the opportunity to watch Mark chart and follow the course that has now led him, and me, to a wedding in Milan. Over the past 14 years, I have shared in his graduation from junior high, high school and college, and have come to consider him my other son. During the summer of 1988, Mark lived in our home in Washington, D.C. Evenings were hot and humid, and like most Washingtonians, the three of us would head for the front porch stoop to sip an iced tea or a beer and share news of the day. That summer was a time when we all had major decisions under consideration—decisions that would require moves to new and untried places. It was on that porch six years ago that Mark first told us of his plans to study in Moscow, and we began to consider a move to Missouri.

Our road to Breakfast Creek was a fairly straight course, and has been a journey taken without regrets. Mark's journey has been longer and less smooth at times, but ultimately it led him to the *Chiesa Sant' Eugenio* (Saint Eugene Church) on 22 *Settembre* 1994 and his marriage to Cinzia.

When Mark first wrote to me about Cinzia, I made a promise to him and to myself to be there (whether "there" was in Los Angeles or Milan) to witness the ceremony—as his friend of many years, as his former teacher, and as his *mama seconda*. When an invitation to their wedding arrived late in August—*Cinzia e Marco annunciano il loro matrimonio*, Concorezzo—I immediately booked a ticket to Italy.

Mark's mother was unable to make the journey, so it was decided that I would represent Mark's family. When the moment to pack finally arrived, I selected a bottle of Breakfast Creek herbal vinegar and a jar of homemade peach and fig chutney from the pantry to take as gifts for *Ottorino* and *Luigia*, Cinza's father and mother. I also packed a few favorite recipes for the groom's dinner Mark and I were planning to prepare in Luigia's *cuchina* (kitchen). My pastry cloth and ingredients for a pumpkin pie (*zucca torta*) were packed along with a bottle of champagne for the celebratory meal on the eve of the wedding.

The week that followed my arrival was *bellissimo* for six wonderful days, I was immersed in lively Italian conversations. I pulled vocabulary from the dusty recesses of my foreign language memory file and mixed in any language that came to mind if my whisper of Italian failed to materialize—Thai, French, English, whatever language I could muster. Late in the week Mark, Cinzia and I drove on the Autostrada to Venice, keeping our speed at between 65–75 miles an hour. When cars passed us at 90–100 miles an hour speeds, Mark explained that Italians drive like they speak—*staccato e rapido*.

Meals from Luigia's kitchen were fresh and light, eaten at a pace that was *rapido* when the pasta was hot and *lentemente* (slowly) when the *formaggio* (cheese) course was served and a second bottle of wine from Ottorino's wine cellar was being uncorked. That was always the point in the meal when my comprehension of spoken Italian was at its sharpest and my ability to make myself understood seemed to be at its best.

The morning of the wedding, Cinzia was dressed by her mother as is the tradition in Italy, and a close friend arranged her hair. Mark and I visited with guests downstairs until the moment arrived for everyone to drive in a caravan to Concorezzo's small 700-year-old cathedral of this community where Cinzia had grown up. Friends and locals greeted our arrival with spirited wishes for the couple's happiness, and visiting continued in the cobblestone drive until the scheduled time for the ceremony arrived at 11:30 a.m.

All over Italy, bells ring in church towers every half hour, so one hardly ever needs a watch to know what time it is. That morning was no exception. At 11:30 sharp, *Marco* took my arm and walked me down the aisle to the pew reserved for the groom's family. He then stood next to the two ceremonial chairs where he and Cinzia would sit during much of the one-hour Mass that followed. Cinzia and her parents followed, and finally other family and friends took their seats. Throughout the ceremony, the love that these guests carried in their hearts for the wedding couple filled Saint Eugene Church. It was a feeling as rich as the voices of the choir that rose with ancient clarity within the walls of the tiny village church.

Papers were signed and witnessed, pictures were taken, and handfuls of *riso* were thrown at the couple as they stepped into the warm circle of friends waiting outside. Then it was off to the Ristorante Toscano for a seven-course wedding meal that lasted for as many hours—*Risotto ai funghi* (it was mushroom season in Italy), *Gnocchetti al Salmone, Tagliata al pepe* (veal with pepper), and *Misto bosco al gelato* (mixed berries and ice cream), to name just a few of the courses. Pauses were built into the meal service to allow food to settle and palates to be cleared with wine or *acqua minerale*. Between courses, there was visiting among tables, walks through the flower gardens, and finally—just before the dessert courses—a ride across the Adda River on a barge designed by Leonardo daVinci. The celebration was a progressive meal that stretched happily into the early evening hours.

Finally it was time for the teacher to toast her student and his bride, and to raise a glass of champagne to the joining of their families across two continents and an ocean. *Marco e Cinzia* are now far from Milan and the family she grew up with. But the small world of Concorezzo has already begun to look outward in the direction of Portland. Plans are being made for the Italians to visit Portland and Milan will always be a second home for Mark and Cinzia.

For me, the journey to Italy will remain a treasured memory of this special young man and his bride, and the hospitality of the Corio family and their wonderful friends. It is a collection of images of grand cities visited—Milan, Bergamo, Monza and Venice—and the piedmont cornfields that stretch across northern Italy. The food, the language, the colors, and the people of Italy are a warm and delicious part of the memories that I brought home with me from a wedding in Milan. (1994)

Back of Beyond

There is a place called Never-Never land that lives in the dreams of all children. It is a bewitching place filled with mystery and benign danger, and of course, a touch of magic. Those who have lived in it and fallen under its strange and wonderful spell never, never want to leave it.

Such a place has long been a part of the lore and language of Australia. For the bushman of the late 18th century, civilization was a constant threat to the old methods and habits that he tenaciously clung to. Ironically, his droving, bullock-punching, and stock-keeping beyond the edges of civilization fueled the very civilization that kept him on the move.

With Australia's gold rush in the mid-1800s came a quadrupling of Australia's population. Railways and settlers drove the bushman out of New South Wales and Queensland and into the Northern Territory—a region of Outback Australia covering about one-sixth of the entire continent.

I have now been to this elusive land of dangers and hardships that bush folk called the Never-Never. It is a tropical land of deserts and torrid tablelands where droughts follow monsoons and the average temperature hovers at 86° F year round. Those unfitted to live in it leave if they are able and swear they will never, never return. But those who fall under its strange spell as I did and come to know its mysteries know that they can never leave it. It will always live in their hearts.

The Northern Territory bush of 1902 was called "the land of plenty of time and wait awhile." It was that place "behind the Back of Beyond," in the "Land of the Never-Never." To experience this world today as I did recently is to understand what Australia and Australians are all about.

In my recent travels through Australia, I met Jane Duncan Owen, a local historian and writer who told me that Aussies refer to their native land as "the Lucky Country." But she reminded me that it has not always been so. For the original 760 convicts sent from England to establish a penal colony in Australia in 1788, this raw continent must have seemed anything but lucky. But over the next 80 years, the labors of 168,000 convicts transformed the Sydney region into one of the most magnificent harbors in the world. Sheep and gold continued to attract settlers in the years after Australia ceased to serve as a penal colony for England.

Charles Darwin noted that transportation had succeeded in transforming vagabonds into useful, hardworking citizens. Australian women were among the first in the world to get the vote, leading Charles Dickens to describe Australia as an egalitarian society—what he wanted England to be.

Australia at the turn of the twentieth century was not yet the egalitarian society that Dickens perceived, but it was a society where hope abounded. Englishmen and women who had historically depended on the sea came to depend on the bush. Pioneer squatters, Bushmen, and cockies (small farmers) were admired by those who lived in towns as the true Australians.

Since so many of the early convicts who built Australia could not read or write, Australia developed a strong oral tradition. Itinerant workers, sheep sheerers, graziers, drovers and Bushmen told colorful stories of bush life around the evening campfires. Sheep dog stories soon grew in Australian lore to the scale of the most outrageous of American fish stories.

Many of the best-loved stories and myths of Australia's bush life were captured in the poems of A. B. Patterson. "Banjo" Patterson lived his early years on a bush station where he learned to ride and met bush characters who later became immortalized in the children's poems and short stories that he published from the late 1890s into the 1930s. Images of early bush life are strong in a poem he called "The Pioneers"—

> *They came of bold and roving stock that would not fixed abide;*
> *They were the sons of field and flock since e'er they learned to ride;*
> *We may not hope to see such men in these degenerate years*
> *As those explorers of the bush—the brave old pioneers.*
> *'Twas they who rode the trackless bush in heat and storm and drought;*
> *'Twas they that heard the master word that called them further out;*
> *'Twas they that followed up the trail the mountain cattle made*
> *And pressed across the mighty range where now their bones are laid....*
>
> (Banjo Patterson, *Favorite Poems*)

But Australia has a much deeper history that Banjo Patterson's poem does not touch on. Long before its relatively recent settlement by Europeans, Australia was populated by nomadic Aboriginals with a rich oral tradition that dates back to the Stone Age. Their stories are of the "Real People," Australia's first pioneers.

Theirs was a life based on the ancient wisdom and philosophy of a culture more than 50,000 years old. It was a simple philosophy based on the idea of living in natural harmony with the plants and animals that existed in their world. That world grew smaller with the expansion of European settlement, forcing Aborigines to try to learn to live in harmony with the land of the Never-Never, the land of the sweet bitter and bitter sweet, the land in Australia's Top End deemed unfit for European settlement.

Today Aborigines make up less than 1% of Australia's population. Like the indigenous people of North America, most now live in urban projects or in remote areas set aside by the government as tribal lands. Alcohol and poverty have clouded their traditional sense of balance with nature and make the survival of their culture uncertain in the coming century.

At the Kakadu Crocodile Hotel in the Northern Territory, I met Abel, a young Aborigine in his 30s whose grandfather was an artist known for his paintings on local rock ledges. Abel spoke with pride of his artist grandfather, and I encouraged him to keep the ancient tradition alive. As I did, he touched his chest with his fist in a gesture of guarding something of the heart. His black hands encircled one of mine as we exchanged goodbyes. A suggestion of alcohol remained in the air where Abel had been after I watched him disappear into a back room bar at the hotel frequented by local Aborigines.

Abel's journey will be a constant balancing act, because he is trying to walk in two different worlds. But for Aborigines who still live as bush folk "behind the Back of Beyond, the Land of Never-Never" is a real place where children never grow up. Land belongs to all things and sharing is the real human way. The "Real People" share their journey by living in harmony with nature because everything is part of the same Oneness.

Time is part of a dimension, which they call "dreamtime". Aborigines believe there was a time before time; there was a time after land appeared, and there is "now." For the nomadic Aboriginal of the Outback bush, life is part of a continuous journey in which dreaming is still going on and the world is still being created. A mass of rocks, a cliff, or a waterfall all represent places we can learn from. And a rock ledge is a canvas on which artists like Abel's grandfather record the message of "dreamtime."

When approaching death, Aborigines celebrate their life. Death is seen as a return to forever, that place where all creatures live without fear. That land they never, never want to leave. That magical place in our dreams located "behind the Back of Beyond." (1995)

Roads Taken

November took a different road this month and ran smack into April. Uncommonly warm temperatures have confused lilacs into thinking they should send buds directly into flower, and migrating swans have been seen down in the Hartsburg Bottoms. One friend identified the five visitors as Tundra swans. Another is sure they must be Trumpeter swans. Whatever they are, they have chosen to take a less traveled route on their annual migration south, and local birdwatchers are enjoying the rare opportunity to observe their curious decision firsthand.

Follow their migratory route one leg beyond the bottoms, and imagine the following scenario. Suppose the five swans decide to drop into Breakfast Creek once they've had their fill of corn and birdwatchers. Would the sudden presence of five huge swans in the quiet world of my homebody geese and ducks make a difference in the lives of our locals down on our pond? Would my ducks and geese be tempted to follow these beauties when they decide to sing their swan song and fly away? Would the local fowl always wonder about bigger ponds beyond their own if they choose to remain behind? Will the day ever come when some deeply ingrained instinct to migrate pulls them away from their comfortable routine lives and safe waters at Breakfast Creek? To finally try their wings? To take to the skies? To hit the road, Jack?

The *road*. It is a common little word that begins softly but gains a strong edge by its end after only four letters. The *road*. A word that emerges with a guttural "r" that has traveled from somewhere at the very back of the throat. From deep in our inner selves. From its anchor in the spirit of individualism and youth that lies deep within each of us.

There is always a road ahead of us and a road behind. The road in front of us is sometimes a tease. Often a challenge. The road behind serves as a reminder of things we once did, and might do again. Roads become the paths we revisit in order to see where we have been, reflect on opportunities taken, and wonder about chances missed.

The road has long been a metaphor for life. Plans made along the way are the road maps we follow, or choose not to follow. Roads may begin in one direction, only to take a totally unexpected turn, leading us to a place not marked on the initial road map. Often, the most memorable journeys are those that follow roads that seem to have no relationship at all to where the journey was intended at the outset of the trip.

Like a road, life is lined with detours, caution signs, full stops, flashing lights, and strategically placed rest stops. It can move at the leisured pace of a back country road or slip into a fast track with wide expanses of highway for shifting gears, passing maneuvers, maximum speed, and direct access. Making choices comes with the territory. A straight and narrow path is the most commonly recommended course in life, but not necessarily the most satisfying to follow. The very predictable nature of its course can become monotonous and cause some to doze at the wheel.

Forks, intersections, and crossroads are more interesting. While straight stretches of road may all run together in our memory, we remember the intersections in our lives in great detail. They are the places where something happened, or we were faced with making a choice—a prospect that is exciting to some and frightening for others. Most memorable are the forks in a road that offer two divergent paths—one familiar, one unknown. When we follow caution, the road not taken has a nagging way of reappearing when we reflect on the direction our life has gone. When we follow our hearts, the road can become a pathway for exploration.

The road is all about decisions we make in life. Roads not taken are songs left unsung. The boy who failed to notice you, and the dance you never danced with him. The road is a city left unexplored. A mountain never climbed. A friend you failed to extend a hand to. It is the talents within each of us left untapped. Healing words left unspoken. Poetry never given a voice. Stories that are never written.

Roads taken at critical intersections of time can make all the difference in how the stories of our lives unfold. In 1935, the Red Rock Lakes National Wildlife Refuge was created in Montana to save the last 73 Trumpeter swans known to exist in the wild. Today, some 14,000 of these birds, once on the road to extinction, range as far north as Alaska and have even been spotted in places as exotic to their normal haunts as southern Boone County in Missouri.

I am at a fork in the road much like the one Robert Frost encountered and immortalized in his poem, *The Road Not Taken*.

> "Two roads diverged in a wood, and I—
> I took the one less traveled by,
> And that has made all the difference."
> [Robert Frost, *The Road Not Taken*]

Breakfast Creek, my base and anchor point, is located along an old stretch of highway less traveled these days than most. In the metaphorical sense, it is a place in my life where two roads have diverged. It is where, in an effort to follow a path anchored deep within myself, I now face choices that may lead me to a road I have only recently begun to travel—a road filled with possibilities as yet untested.

For me, writing is the road. Each story begins with a single word. Words collected become threads. Threads are woven together and each story's telling becomes a journey. Each week as I launch off in a new direction, I wonder just where the journey will lead me. That is part of the mystery and allure that comes with taking the road less traveled.

Over the past years, "Notes From Breakfast Creek" has allowed me space to explore worlds both near and distant, and to share their poetry and stories. As another Thanksgiving approaches and my head fills with images of December on the horizon, I realize that taking this writing road has made all the difference in my life. (1997)

Chapter Nine

A Writer's Imagination

A Good Pen and a Cup of Coffee

The Girl in the Picture

Quiet Places

The Red Shoes

Travel Across Time

Finding E. B. White

Images of Sand and Saffron

Havana Dreaming

Documenting My Conversation with Denzel

A Good Pen and a Cup of Coffee

In recent years, I have grown to love a good fountain pen. I remember having one years ago when I was a high school student, but carrying around a bottle of ink wasn't convenient. School desks in the 1950s, even into the 1960s, still had a hole in the upper right-hand corner of the desktop, designed to receive an inkwell. But by then, the wells had gone dry. Cartridges and ballpoint pens were in.

A fountain pen has an altogether different feel in the hand than a ballpoint or disposable rolling writer pen. My pen is a Sailor—black and honey-colored tortoise shell floating in Lucite, with a gold nib and band. An hour of writing, pen point floating on liquid as it meets paper, empties the pen's reservoir. Each time I start to write, I begin by immersing my pen into one of several glass ink bottles on my desk. It is part of the ceremony of writing. For words to flow, ink must flow first. The pen must be ready to meet the page. As I look at my bottle of Quink Parker black ink, I realize that all of the words that I create this morning are floating in that glass bottle. Like a nomad whose travels are tied to the next oasis for water, I am drawn to these inkwells in my thirst for words.

The pen unscrews, revealing an empty ink chamber. With a twisting motion of the end of the pen, an interior mechanism descends to draw up the ink and the words. After a period of staring beyond pen and page, out spill the words. The whole business of writing seems a bit like magic when you think of the trip each word has to make before it takes shape on a page.

Words flow most easily when we feel passionately about something and sense the need to express that passion. For some, expression finds its way out through spoken words or strong actions. For me, expression comes through writing. Like Ada in the film, *The Piano*, my pen is my piano. And like the piano, writing becomes stronger and more satisfying the more it is practiced. It is a conversation we have with ourselves, a way of thinking about and expressing our feelings.

Writing as a form of expression has not disappeared, but it has become less personal, less passionate, and less frequently the mode taken. I am not speaking of novels or books of poetry. I am referring more to correspondences between friends and to journal writing—the forms of expression that take the most time and effort to record. It is easier to reach a friend on the telephone than it is to write. But I wonder if the message is the same.

At Christmas time, Kit and I received a basketful of cards, many simply signed with no accompanying message, others with a Xeroxed inclusion chronicling in great detail the sender's past year. We found that most often the cards that we talked about were ones where the friend had taken the time to pen a note, however brief. It was that personal touch that gave the card meaning. For that very reason, we never send a card without writing a personal note. It takes time, but it makes all the difference.

As a child, I remember decorating a shoe box for Valentine's Day and putting it on my desk at school. During the day, classmates secretly dropped heart-shaped notes into each box, with personal messages penned the night before. That early tradition of exchanging romantic notes was an important part of my growing up that continues to this day. One romantic poem is worth a thousand roses or boxes of chocolates, because it comes from the heart. Few things touch the heart like a poem from another's heart, whether romantic or silly. My favorite Valentine message this month came from a friend whose handwriting is so distinctive that a signature was not necessary. It read:

> *I waited lonely as a cloud*
> *Standing on the roof top (late)*
> *My head was bloody but unbowed*
> *I reconciled me to my fate*
> *Atop the Empire State.*
> *Where were you?*

When I was a child, my grandmother became my secret pal. Greeting cards with secret messages grew into letters filled with thoughts and news of what was going on in our lives. It was a correspondence that continued for more than forty years across thousands of miles. Our letters became an ongoing conversation that kept us connected through our thoughts during long periods of separation. With the passing of my secret pal, I am working at keeping the tradition of writing letters alive with my nephews, Christopher and Adam, and my godson, Davy.

Maintaining a correspondence with friends requires time and careful attention, like keeping a cup of coffee hot. Not just warm, which it becomes the minute cream is added, but hand-warming hot from the top of the cup to the bottom. The real trick is in sitting still. Doing just that one thing. Focusing on just that cup of coffee or on finding the right word.

A writing life, like that cup of coffee, is richer and more satisfying if you work at keeping it hot, work on maintaining the right balance of cream to coffee. Writing with a good fountain pen is rather like the difference between drinking a cup of coffee from a diner mug (mine is from the Moose Cafe) and a Styrofoam cup. It takes more time to wash the ironware mug than it does to toss the disposable cup, but I guarantee it will be a better cup of coffee every time.

Get a hot cup of coffee and pick up a pen that you like. Then work on sitting still. If you listen to yourself long enough, the words will spill out of your pen, and you will have taken the first step to adding writing to your life. The pen, the ink, and the coffee are merely part of the ceremony. Ultimately, you have to sit still long enough to allow writing to happen. There is poetry in each of us. Writing is a way to give that poetry a voice. When it happens, it is a rich experience, indeed.
(1994)

The Girl in the Picture

In the gray morning chill at Breakfast Creek, I walked to our pond and reflected on another time. Saigon, October 1969. I had flown there from Bangkok to visit a friend and spent a week exploring the city's bustling streets on my own. In the pond's reflection, I recalled the words of a letter that I wrote to my parents after that trip.

"Dear Mom and Dad—Saigon feels quite safe, at least at the present time. Much to my surprise, it hardly appears touched by the war. Completely charming and French in design, with beautiful Catholic cathedrals and wide, tree-lined boulevards alive with sidewalk cafés, outdoor food markets, and even an opera house. The mix of French and Vietnamese in both the language and food is utterly delicious.

"I am sitting now on the verandah of the Continental Palace Hotel, sipping a lemonade and marveling at the elegance of Vietnamese women as they move through the bustling traffic. Their beauty seems unruffled as they ride sidesaddle on the backs of noisy, exhaust-spewing motor scooters, dressed in pastel silk *ao dai*, the traditional dress of Vietnamese women. The street noise is deafening.

"There are, of course, signs of war. Barbed wire, sandbags piled around guard posts at South Vietnamese and U.S. military billets and government offices. President Thieu's Palace is fortified by an entire army unit. The streets are always filled with military jeeps, trucks, cars, bicycles, taxis, and motorcycles with sidecars—all roaring along in a mass of noxious fumes.

"You could almost forget about the war if you just stayed in Saigon. This city of many faces, once referred to as 'the Paris of the East,' still tries to maintain its once elegant grace. After all, life must go on. But at night, when the city finally settles down, the sound of gunfire heard in the distance reminds everyone that the war is less than thirty miles away.

"After a week in Saigon, I flew to Phnom Penh (the capital of Cambodia). Because it was only a 25-minute flight, the pilot flew quite low over the rice paddy landscape. From the outskirts of Saigon to the Cambodian border, large brown pockmarks on the earth traced the progress of the war across the rural countryside. Then suddenly, we entered another world. Like Saigon, Phnom Penh felt very French, but it was incredibly quiet and slow moving by comparison. Nowhere in

Asia have I experienced a country so innocent, so seemingly untouched by time or war."

When I look up from that momentary reflection at our pond's edge, I realize that 27 years and a million lifetimes have passed since I penned that letter. Cruise ships now bring tourists to Hanoi and there are probably KFC and McDonalds franchisees mixed in with the traditional Vietnamese food stalls along its city boulevards. Cambodia as I saw it in that magical window of time in the late '60s no longer exists. The memory of its killing fields is still a painful wound as yet unhealed. Yet, deep in the human spirit, there is always hope.

Another reflection surfaces. A rural road, somewhere outside of Saigon, 1972. A war photographer's camera captures forever the horrifying image of a little girl running with her arms held above her head. A look of terror is frozen on her face. Napalm has burned through the girl's clothes and into the skin on her bare arms and back. She is naked. For the world, she became "the girl in the picture" that we cannot forget.

Where is she now? I wondered, looking deep into the water. Then the answer came. The girl in the picture is Kim Fook. She is now 34 years old, the mother of a little boy not yet three who can count in Vietnamese, English and Spanish. On the streets of Toronto where Kim Fook lives today, she is able to walk unnoticed in a crowd. Long sleeves hide the story of the scars above her wrists and on her back. She admits that the scars are highly sensitive to cold temperatures, but considers Toronto her home now.

She remembers crying once when she saw a beautiful girl in Saigon in a short-sleeved *ao dai*. She also remembers wanting to be a doctor. But her family had moved to Tay Ninh Province where someone recognized her as the girl in the picture. Instead of medical school, she was given a secretarial job by the government and visiting journalists were brought often to see her. When she again applied to medical school in Saigon, the government confiscated her educational records.

Eventually, she began to follow the teachings of Baptist missionaries and finally obtained permission to study in Cuba, where she met and married a fellow Vietnamese student. On their flight back to Vietnam, the plane stopped briefly in Toronto. In those few minutes, the couple made a decision that has changed the direction of their lives. They got off the plane and applied to the Canadian government for political asylum.

Looking for a final time into the pond, I see the National Mall in Washington, D.C. It is Veteran's Day, 1996. A black granite wall cuts deeply into the raw earth. At its apex where grass is growing, Maya Lin is lying in the grass with her eye right at the top of the wall. From this spot, the young architect who designed the Vietnam Veterans Memorial in 1982, explains why this is her favorite vantage point. "From here you can see two reflections that connect the wall to history. On one side of the wall is a reflection of the Washington Monument. On the other, the Lincoln Memorial."

For the millions of Americans who visit the memorial each year, the Wall has provided a way for them to finally come to grips with a war that deeply divided the nation a quarter of a century ago. Etched into black granite are the names of the war's 58,000 dead. By design, the names are small, pulling you to the Wall. To touch, and be touched, by each of the names and the memory that their collective death reflects.

On this day, a small woman is standing at the Wall with her son. She tries to explain to him that this war happened in the place where she was born, at a time when she was not much older than he is now. The boy reaches out and runs his small fingers across the names etched into the polished granite surface in front of him. The woman returns to her own thoughts.

In her reflection, time dissolves and the woman sees herself as a little girl again, running with her arms held above her head. One day, she thinks to herself, she must tell her son the story of the girl in the picture and the war. But on this particular day, she prefers to be just one among the many who have come to the Wall … to touch … to be touched … and finally, to forgive. (1996)

Quiet Places

For each of us, there are times when it is necessary to get away from the noise of the world. To move toward silence, toward a quiet place where we hope to be able to hear ourselves think. Once there, we must learn to listen to silence. To hear what it has to say to us.

Abraham Lincoln's quiet place was the last pew at the back of St. John's Episcopal Church, located just a block from the White House. It was a place where Lincoln could sit unnoticed and seek guidance through one of America's darkest dramas. A quiet place where he could find peace of mind in a world where peace seemed a distant dream.

Ulysses S. Grant, never comfortable in his role as President, chose the lobby of the old Willard Hotel as his place for quiet anonymity. Washington lore has it that Grant would slip out of the White House alone, walk to the Willard, find an empty chair along the hotel's long lobby, and light up a cigar. Before long, politicians seeking his favor began to hang out in the same lobby. Unable to sit unnoticed in the crowd, President Grant fled the "dammed lobbyists" who continue to this day to be an active part of Washington politics and its landscape.

I taught for a number of years at a school in Los Angeles that was blessed with a very talented modern dance teacher named Bill Allen. Bill's place for reflection was in his windowless urban classroom. After the last student had gone home, he would turn out the lights, surround himself with quiet and meditate in total darkness. It was there, in that solitary setting that he found the energy he needed to continue inspiring 120 kids a day at this inner city junior high school.

For me, those teaching days were filled with energy demands that were as rewarding as they were exhausting. A day spent dealing with the needs and noise level of an urban campus of 2,000 junior high students, followed by a half hour to forty-five minute commute on the busy leg of the Santa Monica Freeway left little space for quiet. It was only when I returned late in the afternoon to our canyon cottage in the Santa Monica Mountains, a quiet world tucked away from the noise of the day, that I found the quiet places I needed to round out my life. My rose garden taught me patience and sharpened my awareness of how nature works her magic; and our small cottage kitchen was the space where I shook off the day's frustrations and began planning strategies for the school day to follow.

Each of us needs a quiet place of our own where we can go to reflect on events in our lives. Even in the generous space that southern Boone County allows those of us lucky enough to live here, there are times when we need to be in a place that allows us to see where we have been, and perhaps catch a glimpse of where we need to go with our lives. Such places are for some people an actual geographic location. A point on the map of their personal world reserved for reflection. For others, they are places in the heart or the mind.

From my writing table at Breakfast Creek, I find myself listening to the sounds of a late January Missouri morning that is wrapped in a blanket of dense fog. Listening makes me aware of the underlying sounds that a quiet house makes—an occasional creak, the furnace kicking on, our lazy black Lab sinking deeper into sleep. After listening for a while, my own thoughts become loud enough for me to hear. Recent conversations that I've had with friends about Hartsburg come to mind, conversations centered around Hartsburg's old grocery store building on Second Street. We bemoan the loss of the town's post office building damaged in last year's "Great Flood of '93" and the coming demise of the MFA brick building. So much of Hartsburg's old architectural character forever gone.

Wouldn't it be grand, the conversation goes, if the community could figure out a way to hang on to the old building that was Connie and Marjorie Barner's grocery store, to preserve it as a part of Hartsburg's past while developing it into a vital place for the town's future. We let our imaginations run with the thought and envision the community spirit that lived during flood times at the Firehouse Cafe rekindled in the old grocery store's cast iron stove. Coffee there would always be hot, lunch tables and a deli counter would be open again for business, and banter would be free for all those who came in to share news or read a newspaper. Regulars would drink their coffee from a personalized coffee mug kept for them on a cup hook behind the counter. There would be space for a lending library and a children's reading corner (with pint-sized chairs), bins of local produce and displays of handmade crafts, a corner housing Hartsburg's history in photos and memorabilia, and upstairs in the old vaudeville theater space, there might even be assorted dance, exercise, and handicraft classes.

The conversation turns next to spring and how much better everything will look when there is finally grass again in Hartsburg. We talk about a spring celebration where everyone brings flowers and bulbs to be planted around town, and a barbecue fundraiser and street dance to help with town flood repairs.

I can imagine such conversations from my quiet writing place, but I know that like a community barn raising, it would take all of us to make it happen and make it work. And there is still a lot of winter left and hard days of thankless work to be done by those directly affected by last summer's floods. This thought takes me back to that lone farmer in Hartsburg who I wrote about recently. Orion Beckmeyer is still bulldozing dirt into the big blew hole near the levee at the end of Bush Landing Road. I wonder what he thinks about all day as he coaxes that old two-cylinder Allis Chalmers dozer back and forth, repeating the motion for hours on end. There is a good chance that on some of the raw, windy January days that Orion has spent out there alone, he wondered why his farming world has been literally turned upside down.

I leave you with this thought. It seems to be a time to listen to the needs of a community still dealing with repairs and the realities of all that must be done to return life to what it was before the 1993 flood. It is time for each of us to let the quiet heroes of Hartsburg know that we are grateful that they go out day after day and work to restore the community. Perhaps, the next time you are in your own quiet place thinking, you will let that thinking prod you to get up and do something. We can all do more to help move Hartsburg along on its road to recovery. After all, that is what community spirit is all about. (1994)

The Red Shoes

A conversation begins to take shape in my garden. I have gone there in the cool of the early morning hours to collect my thoughts and harvest snow peas. Moving squat-legged between the rows, I weed the base of the pea plants while my eyes search for green pods hanging between the leaves. It is an exercise in quiet concentration, a bit like trying to find a chameleon in a forest. The eye learns to look for snowy traces of the white flower from which each pea emerges. Delicate reminders of the ongoing cycle of life.

I am never alone in my garden. Four cats immediately find me and stretch out on the cool earth to watch me as I weed. Soon, four tails move up and down in sync with the rhythm of my breathing. "In my past life, I was a cat," I tell them. There is no reaction or change of expression on their stoic faces. The slow rising and falling of the four tails creates a soft rustle in the golden straw lining the narrow pathway through the pea vines. They are meditating, I realize. Like my own thoughts, theirs are a thousand miles away.

I turn the corner and begin to work my way up between the peas and a mounded row of strawberry plants. Runners have grown out laterally from the long, straight berry row. At the end of each runner, new emerging plants have begun to root themselves in the straw. The runners connect my thoughts to David Guterson's *Snow Falling on Cedars*, a novel set in the Pacific Northwest in the early 1950s. Then to the Japanese-American strawberry farmers in the story who settled on a small island in Puget Sound before World War II.

"I should cut off the new growth and begin a second row of plants," I thought to myself. That is what Kabuo learned as a child, working on his father's seven acre strawberry farm. Then Pearl Harbor changed everything, and everyone, on the island in ways that could not have been imagined. A murder trial and a snowstorm brought the island to a standstill and forced its inhabitants to come face to face with the depths of their own prejudice.

In my garden, the novel's quietly emerging human struggle, told through the poetic metaphor of snow falling on cedars, carries me forward to a conversation—one that has been quietly taking shape as I've gardened this morning. An artist, a writer, and a political activist are having a conversation in a garden. The three women are talking easily as friends do, although we have only just met in a blink of my imagination. I am telling Aung San Suu Kyi, a striking Burmese woman in her early 50s, the story of how I first met Maxine three years ago while visiting artist Claude Monet's garden in Giverny, a small village north of Paris.

What connects our distant lives is the shared need for a garden. After all, isn't it in a garden that this imaginary conversation is taking place? The garden belongs to Maxine. Suu Kyi, the 1991 Nobel Peace Prize winner and leader of Burma's opposition democracy movement, is admiring the giant red poppies that Maxine has planted in her garden. The Oriental poppy is a flower familiar to the diminutive political activist, still thin from her six years of house arrest ordered by the country's military junta in 1990. Suu Kyi comments that this garden reminds her of Burma.

Sitting at a small round table in the center of Maxine's garden, Suu Kyi's thoughts drift to the narrow bench under a garden window—a favorite spot to sit on at her banquette against a garden window, a favorite place to sit in her lakeside residence in Rangoon. "The generals," she says softly, "have renamed Rangoon *Yangon* and the country became Myanmar when they took control in 1988. No one asked the Burmese if they wanted to change the name of the country. To the people who believe in democracy, it is still Burma."

Sitting in Maxine's garden, Suu Kyi looks like a delicate flower herself. There is a spray of orchids where she has pulled back her hair. An occasional strand of gray in her otherwise black hair reminds me of the strain of her continuing struggle to be heard. In a pink silk blouse and an elegant *longyi* skirt, she seems both relaxed and controlled. "The red of this poppy is a color we celebrate," Suu Kyi tells us. "Just last month, I laughed and clapped while members of my National League for Democracy Party danced in my garden to 'The Red Baron,' the national anthem of my father's independence movement against the British at the end of World War II. He was assassinated when I was only two. I must now finish what he began."

Later, the three of us go into Maxine's studio where my artist friend begins to paint Suu Kyi. On the wall is a painting of two dancers. One of the dancers is wearing a lime green dress and a pair of red high-heeled shoes. "Perhaps that is me," Suu Kyi says, laughing softly. "In life, I dance each day with danger; and yet, I feel invincible. From now on, when people ask me where I get the strength to continue leading Burma's democratic struggle, I will tell them that it comes from the red shoes."

As the image of Suu Kyi begins to emerge on Maxine's canvas, she talks about her life as Burma's most famous activist. To the military junta, she is the evil sorceress in their nightmare. To the Burmese, she is their adored queen of hearts. Though she has, for the time being, been freed from house arrest, Suu Kyi continues to live alone at an aging villa where the memories of its once beautiful gardens keep her spirit alive. "In what remains of my garden," she tells us, "I search for the strength that I will need one day to lead the people of Burma."

In Rangoon every Saturday and Sunday at 4 p.m., Suu Kyi climbs onto a table behind her front gate at 54 University Avenue. From there, she can be seen by the thousands of people who gather each weekend and risk arrest to hear The Lady, as she is called by her followers, speak out against policies of the present military government.

"My struggle is a lonely one," Suu Kyi adds "but it is one I cannot abandon. I am free to leave Burma today, return to my family in England and go dancing every night. But my heart would remain in Rangoon, in the garden where I stand each weekend and speak to my followers."

I am back in my own garden now. The early morning coolness is gone and the four cats have moved into the shade. As I stand up at the end of the row of strawberries that I have just weeded, I notice my feet. I am wearing a pair of red rubber gardening clogs. I smile as I think of my imagined conversation with Maxine and Aung San Suu Kyi. Then, clicking my heels together like Dorothy, I head down a path of yellow straw and out of the garden. I walk back to the house feeling invincible in my red shoes, ready to meet the challenges of the days that lie ahead. (1996)

Travel Across Time

This fall, Missouri is swimming in a sweet surfeit of apples. Kind neighbors with groaning apple trees are calling friends with offers of free fruit. Their generosity has led to a flourish of pie making, apple juicing, chutney canning, and apple saucing activities in our kitchen, all of which begin with peeling, coring, and slicing. As I begin to peel apples picked yesterday in a neighbor's orchard, I tune in to the sounds around me. Kittens chase dry leaves across the front porch. An occasional car passes by. A fat black walnut the size of an orange hits the barn's corrugated roof with a solid *thunk*.

Then a distant whistle carried on a breeze enters the kitchen window. I am aware that it is a sound known from other worlds and earlier times. Solitary and transient, it can be heard above the familiar rhythms of Breakfast Creek. A train moving freight along the river bluffs of the Missouri River ten miles away captures my attention. At that moment, apple peeling moves into automatic pilot. I am free to begin my own mental journey.

There is something magical about the idea of traveling by train. Perhaps it is the connection to distant places or a romantic nostalgia for bygone eras. For me, it comes from somewhere in my childhood. Memories of a first train trip from New England to Washington, D.C., 40 years ago. For a ten-year old, it was filled with sounds and motion and mystery that to this day carry me instantly to other places and times.

On a sleeper train somewhere in Northeast Thailand, I am en route from Bangkok to the river town where I will cross the Mekong River and enter Laos. I love the night seen through an open train window. The smell of wood fires in passing rural villages and lights that dance in distant hills like lanterns hanging from a string. The *clickity clack* of the train's steel wheels riding the curve of the track rock me in and out of sleep.

The scene changes to Gare Saint-Lazare Station in Paris. It is the turn of the century and Impressionist artist Claude Monet boards the train with his wife, Alice. After spending a few days in Paris, they are returning to their home in the village of Giverny. It is winter and the great iron horse leaves the grand Paris station enveloped in a billowing cloud of white steam.

Ninety years later, Kit and I take a train from the same station on a crisp October day, bound for an afternoon in Monet's home and gardens. We have brought a picnic of French bread from a local *boulangerie*, an assortment of cheeses and apples, licorice and bottles of spring water. The journey is through familiar canvases painted by the artist a century ago. Only the steam is missing.

Another journey thirty years ago moves me through a Japanese landscape. Speed and efficiency is the engine that drive this densely populated island nation. Japan's computerized Bullet train is an automated wonder. Looking like a pencil sharpened at both ends, the high-speed train arrives on time and on a dime. Doors open, masses exit, others press in, doors close, and the bullet takes flight— all in the course of a minute's time.

When the doors of the train reopen, I am in Madrid's Atocha station en route to Segovia's great Roman aqueducts. Looking up momentarily, light moves across Breakfast Creek, carrying me across another decade of time back to Italy's sun-washed, rustic countryside. There I happily enter a Tuscan landscape that appears untouched by the passage of trains or time.

Journeys as yet untaken also move across my mind. In the summer of 1988, I received information from a travel office in New York promoting a nostalgic rail odyssey from Paris to Hong Kong. Fifteen royal blue and gold cars from the famed Orient Express (restored to their original late 1920s grandeur) were to depart from Lyon Station in Paris, bound for an 18-day sojourn to Hong Kong along one of the world's longest and most spectacular routings. For $20,000 per person, with a limit of 30 participants each from North America, Asia, and Europe, we too could be a part of history.

The promotional packet was a delicious read. I browsed through the maps and the trip's itinerary. It would begin with a welcoming party at the Hotel de Crillon in Paris. Sightseeing in Reims to be followed by a champagne lunch in the cellar of Mumm Cordon Rouge. Then high tea in Potsdam and an Orient Express Ball at the Grand Hotel Berlin (east). Tables in the two dining carriages are set with china, silver, crystal and linen, and master chefs will create gourmet meals featuring regional cuisines along the way.

In Warsaw, there is a Chopin concert. Then on to Brest, Moscow, and the long journey across Siberia to Novosibirsk. At Irkuktsk, a stop is planned with an excursion by hydrofoil on Lake Baikal. Crossing the Russian border at Zabikalsk, the train enters China at Manchouli before heading on to Beijing and a visit to the Great Wall. Then a day on to Hong Kong, and an Orient Express Gala Farewell Ball. But, alas, that train will be leaving without me.

I am now back in the kitchen capturing sliced apples under a layer of pie dough. I may never see the inside of the famed Orient Express, but I love revisiting train excursions from my past and dreaming of exotic journeys that might someday happen. For those who daydream, the ride is free. "Just hear that whistle blowing … All aboard! Care to come along?"(1997)

Finding E. B. White

Recently, the *New York Times* reviewed a reissued collection of essays by E.B. White, first published in 1942. The essays were written during a period when White moved his family from Manhattan to a salt-water farm in Maine, a move analogous to the urban-to-rural migration that Kit and I made in 1988 from Washington, DC, to Breakfast Creek—our own small farmlet in southern Boone County, Missouri.

Kit and I were in New York when I read the review. I immediately jotted down the title, *One Man's Meat*, in a small notebook that I carry with me for such notations. When I am in any major city, exploring bookstores is as much a part of my daily diet as reading the *Times* is for a New Yorker. My habit is not to return from my travels with a suitcase filled with new clothes and shoes. Rather, I stock up on books that are then stacked on a table next to our reading chairs, in the same way canned foods are stored in a pantry. One by one, they are consumed as time allows, providing food for thought throughout each coming season.

But, back to E.B. White. Why the interest in a man who wrote essays for *The New Yorker* and *Harper's Magazine* seventy years ago? Perhaps you are thinking I must have him confused with another E.B. White who wrote children's books. Could this be the same essayist who wrote *Charlotte's Web*—one of the best-loved children's classics of all time? What would an urbane Manhattanite know about pigs and barns and spiders anyway?

That same day in New York City, our son Hayden accompanied us on a leisurely stroll along Madison Avenue and down a stretch of 5th Avenue. As we approached 47th Street, I suggested a detour through the Diamond District. "I'm looking for a gem of another kind," I told Hayden. "Ever been to the Gotham Bookmart & Gallery? No? Well, you're in for a rare treat."

Buried deep within the long block of 47th Street between 5th Avenue and the Avenue of the Americas is a small bookstore surrounded on all sides by commerce and pedestrian congestion on a scale that can be overwhelming and exhausting for the casual stroller. For those lucky enough to stumble upon and go down the Gotham Bookstore's easy-to-miss stairwell, a sea of calm instantly replaces the frenetic street level world of Hassidic Jewish diamond traders and discount jewelry marts that one must wade through to get there. But it is a trek that serious book lovers have gladly undertaken since the bookstore's doors opened almost 90 years ago.

As I stopped to adjust my pace from street hustle to library halt, two postcards displayed on the store's cluttered checkout counter caught my eye. One was a black and white photograph taken during a 1948 reception held in the very space we had just entered. Seated in the virtually unchanged surroundings of crowded bookshelves were W. H. Auden, Tennessee Williams, Gore Vidal, and a host of other well-known writers in the NYC literary scene at that time. I did not see E. B. White and wondered for a moment why. Perhaps he was still living in Maine on the farm he and his family had moved to ten years earlier.

The second postcard was of the Gotham's back room where a desk was piled with books ready for shelving. Draped across the desk and perched in lofty rarified open spaces in the bookcases behind the desk were three longhaired, yellow tabbies. Each cat sported a white sock or two and a white underbelly. Literary cats, it seems, have long been a tradition at the Gotham, as they were at Ernest Hemingway's home in Key West and Havana, Cuba. It wasn't long before I found one in the backroom sprawled under a lamp on the very desk I had just seen in the postcard.

This being the first cat I had seen since our arrival in Manhattan, I couldn't pass by without rubbing its ears and running my hand through its warm yellow fur. "Where can I find a copy of E. B. White's essays?" I asked the docile old reference cat. "I prefer T.S. Eliot's verses, myself," the resident cat purred, "but if you have your heart set on the essayist, look in the front bookshelf at floor level." The cat never moved a whisker, and it was only as I turned to leave that I detected the slightest suggestion of interest in the subject of my search.

"A cat person should know that floor level is where one finds authors whose names come at the tail end of the alphabet. Being a literary cat, I rub up against the 'Ws' regularly, and White's books have been around for longer than I've lived here. Ever read his book about a little pig and a spider? What was her name, anyway? Rather a strange name for a common barn spider, wouldn't you say? Charlotte, wasn't it?"

Following the cat's directions, I found what I had been looking for. In the book's introduction, E. B. White described the essays as reflections from the pastoral period of his life, a time when he was "a man in search of the first person singular." Though he loved New York, he felt restless, obsessed by weekly deadlines, and "stuck in the editorial 'we'." The farm and barn he owned in Maine confronted White with new challenges and surrounded him with new acquaintances. And, not surprisingly, many of the characters in his barnyard later appeared in *Charlotte's Web*.

I am now back at Breakfast Creek. Each day, I treat myself to an EBW essay while I have my morning coffee on the front porch. Sometimes, I read them aloud to the cats and kittens napping around my feet or perched in precarious postures along the porch railing. "Once in everyone's life," White wrote of his life on the farm, "there is apt to be a period when one is fully awake, instead of half asleep. I think of those five years in Maine as the time when this happened to me."

For me, E. B. White is a kindred spirit. Each day on his farm was filled with moments of "seeing, feeling, and listening as a child sees, feels and listens." And though more than sixty years have passed, his wit and wisdom have endured. In closing, I leave you with a classic EBW witticism:

"The egg has been an enduring theme in my life, and I have allowed my small flock of laying hens to grow old in service. Cosmetically they leave much to be desired, but their ovulation is brisk, and I greet them with the same old gag when I enter the pen: "White here. Cubism is dead." (EBW) (1997)

Images of Sand and Saffron

Leaving the restaurant, I pulled the collar of my coat up around my neck. At that same moment, the moon fell toward my feet. The tiny crescent of silver had nearly touched the ground when a hand reached out of the dark and caught it. "Your earring," a man whispered before handing the silver ornament to me and disappearing into the night.

The image of the moon connected the intersections that I had passed through that evening. Emerging from the Rasoi, a local Indian restaurant, I had stepped into the cold winter air of a moonlit Missouri. At the same moment, my thoughts had been captured by the epic drama of Count Laszlo de Almásy and Katharine Clifton. By their passionate journey from Gilf Kebir in the North African desert to the maze-like world they negotiated through in Cairo's bazaars. By images of prehistoric swimmers on the walls of a cave discovered during a desert expedition. By characters humming dance music from the late 1930s.

"I'll be looking at the moon, but I'll be seeing you."

Still captured by the images drifting like sand across my mind, I had tilted my head back to look up at the moon. In that slight movement, the thin silver loop holding a crescent-shaped earring in my ear had been pushed free by the fur that lines my silken coat the color of saffron. "Your coat looks Oriental," one of my friends had said just moments before the moon had begun to fall.

"If I gave you my hand, you would drop it, wouldn't you?" Katharine said to Almásy in Michael Ondaatje's novel, *The English Patient*. Almásy did not answer her.

The coat wrapped me in images of Damascus, where Arab merchants who lived in another time sold bolts of silk brought from Baghdad. Brocades and brilliantly colored satins. But prized most by far was the thin silken gauze used to make nightgowns for the heavily veiled, wealthy Muslim women who searched the shops of the bazaars hoping to find a bolt of the gossamer silk that when worn, created the illusion of nakedness. Like the desert, creating images in the shadows.

Five of us had gathered over plates of Indian curry and jasmine rice at the Rasoi to talk about the film version of *The English Patient* that we had just seen. Leaving the theater, it had been hard to breathe. As though we'd been holding our breath for hours. As though we too had been caught in the desert sand storm that had engulfed Katharine and Almásy so suddenly and violently one star-filled desert night, changing the course of their lives forever. As though our own lungs were filled with sand and pain, and, like the dying English patient, held less and less air with each passing day.

"What do you love most?" Almásy asked Katharine after they left the desert and returned to Cairo. "Water," she answered.

When a waiter came to take our order, we were all suddenly thirsty. "Do you have Indian beer?" we asked. "No," he answered. "Honey Wheat, Foster, and Bud Light." We put in our orders and asked for water right away. Before we could talk about the movie's powerful images, we had to wash the sand from our throats and give our lungs time to fill again with air. Then we could return to the desert to retrace the story's epic journey.

"What is the singular most powerful image that you have carried away from the film?" Kit asked the group assembled at our urban oasis. It was a difficult question, for this is a film filled with images painted in desert light and shadows, weaving together missing threads that would finally link the identity of the burned English patient to Almásy and take him back to the Gilf Kebir camp where he first saw Katharine emerge like a willow from a plane the color of a blazing desert sun.

"It has to be the aerial image that opens and ends the film," someone offered. Of Katharine wrapped in a shroud of white parachute silk, being flown in an open plane over shifting dunes in a borderless desert. The plane's small shadow on the sand shifts first to the shape of a woman's back. Then to one of swimmers painted on the walls of the desert cave where Katharine dies in darkness.

The dunes then segue into another time and place. To the year 1944 and the final days of the Second World War in Europe. To an abandoned monastery in Italy where the English patient is being tended by Hana, a young Canadian nurse who is herself a victim of this war that has left deep personal wounds. In an instant of the camera's eye, the deep depressions of desert sand become folds in the white bed sheets of Hana's hopelessly burned charge. There we begin through flashbacks to learn the identity of the mysterious English patient and the fate of Katharine Clifton.

I offer a second image. The thimble filled with saffron that Almásy buys for Katharine in a Cairo bazaar. The thimble he later sees hanging on a delicate silver chain around her neck as he carries her into the Cave of Swimmers following the plane crash. I am back in the present now, and mango ice cream is being served. I use the moment to remove a small yellow pouch from my purse and present it to my friends. It contains a tiny thimble that I had filled earlier that day with threads of Spanish saffron.

"You need add only one or two threads to a pot of rice," I tell my friends. "That is all you need to color and flavor the rice. It is that rich."

Images of sand and saffron. Threads linking us that night when the moon fell to another time and story. To a film rich in images that will play in the mind again and again in the days and weeks that follow. To a novel I first read four years ago quite by accident. I had picked it up in a bookstore because of the image on its cover. The grainy image of a man being enveloped by sand in a desert storm. I opened the book and....

The English Patient. Images of sand and saffron in a dreamlike tale of ill-fated romance. A poetic novel filled with images not soon to be forgotten. (1997)

Havana Dreaming

It's barely winter and already dreams of warm-water ports have begun to visit me in the night. Kit and I are in the *Hotel Inglaterra* in Old Havana in a room overlooking the *Parque Central* and *Gran Teatro*. It is late and the Latin rhythms moving through the walls and window of our room have drawn us to the hotel's upstairs bar. Ruben Gonzalez, the white-haired musician featured in Ry Cooder's documentary film *Buena Vista Social Club*, is at the piano.

I am wearing a slinky lime green dress and red high-heeled shoes. Kit is dressed in tropical white linen. Cubans, I have read, are a proud people. When you go out in the evening, you dress for the occasion. And this is a dream of such an occasion. After concluding a set with "Como Siento Yo," Rubén, who is in his early 80s, circulates gracefully around the room, greeting people with warmth.

When the tall piano player arrives at our table, we ask him to join us. When I ask about Ernest Hemingway's old haunts, Rubén mentions the *Floridita* bar/restaurant two blocks from our hotel. "Papa Hemingway had three passions," the piano player went on to say. "He loved literature, good company, and drinking. His friends were Hollywood movie stars, bullfighters, boxers, politicians, and local people like journalist Fernando Campoamor. He introduced Papa to *El Floridita* while accompanying him on his nocturnal strolls."

The next day, we set out to explore the places Hemingway frequented in *Habana Vieja*, the historic heart of the city. Our first stop is the *Floridita*, a short walk from the *Hotel Inglaterra*. This bar Hemingway immortalized as the "best joint in the Caribbean" in his final novel, *Islands in the Stream*, still has the original red and black décor. We ask where the writer liked to sit and are shown a stool at the far end of the bar with a chain across it. Talking to the bartender, we learn the legend of the daiquiri.

"Daiquiris are made with white rum, refined sugar, lime juice and crushed ice. Hemingway and the *Floridita's* owner, Constante Ribalaigua, invented the drink. Hemingway even had his own version called 'Papa's Special'—a double shot of rum without sugar."

Listening to the bartender's tales, it's clear that Hemingway's favorite haunts in Old Havana, made legendary through his writing, are still lovingly preserved in this city where time has stood still for the past four decades. On the way out, we pass a black and white photograph of Hemingway and a friend with an inscription—"Happy New Year *Floridita* 1951, Gary Cooper and Ernest Hemingway." If the famous pair had walked in the door at that moment and ordered two Papa's Specials, we would not have been at all surprised.

On *Calle Obispo,* we locate the *Hotel Ambos Mundos* where Hemingway stayed off and on between 1936 and 1939. In a simply furnished room, room 511, he wrote *A Farewell to Arms* and part of *For Whom the Bell Tolls.* The hotel remained Hemingway's home away from Key West, Florida until 1940 when the author relocated to Cuba and moved into a large Spanish colonial-style farmhouse nine miles from Havana.

In the dream, Kit and I visit the farmhouse Hemingway shared with several wives (Martha Gellhorn in 1939 and later Mary Welsh until leaving Cuba for the last time in 1960) a steady stream of guests, and fifty-seven cats. From a second story study, the writer could see the distant lights of Havana. Each day, he rose at dawn and wrote sometimes until past midnight, standing in front of his portable Royal typewriter that rested on a shelf.

Hemingway is standing, typing a letter to his wife Mary. "Today is an absolute perfect, cool day; but with fine sun and high clouds and everything looks fresh and new and lovely." Then I wake up. The scene from an upstairs window at Breakfast Creek is unmistakably wintry—a cold, gray day with snow still plastered against tree branches and ice covering the road.

That morning, we drive to Ashland and spend two hours working out at Superior Fitness on Broadway. With the arrival of winter and Kit's recent retirement after 40 years of teaching, we've decided to re-tone our bodies and get some serious aerobic exercise over the next three months.

While treadmilling, I tune out the soap opera drama on the TV screens and let my thoughts drift off in search of warm breezes to a hilltop villa near Havana that is surrounded by palms, mango trees and hibiscus. In the drawing room, Ava Gardner, Gary Cooper and Ingrid Bergman are engrossed in a conversation with a famous bullfighter. Across the room, a tall woman in a slinky lime green dress and red high heels is watching the owner of the house prepare a round of Papa Specials. (2003)

Documenting My Conversation with Denzel

There he was. Standing next to me on the porch of the Sundance Institute's Tree Room Restaurant, waiting for a break in the rain. He'd just finished dining with a group of young actors attending a Sundance Institute workshop. Robert Redford, the independent film institute's founder, was still inside, engrossed in a conversation at his favorite table. Denzel Washington who Redford had brought in to mentor a handful of aspiring directors had just left another table to step out into the night air. Pausing when he saw the rain, the actor moved next a tall woman with red hair.

The rain continued. Denzel had recently starred in *The Hurricane*, a movie about a boxer for which he did a considerable amount of training in preparation for action scenes in the ring. I could tell that he had, though I chose not to say as much. Instead, the two of us continued to let the steady rhythm of the falling rain fill the silence that hung heavy in the night air.

That evening, I didn't tell Denzel that I taught for 12 years in South Central Los Angeles, a neighborhood the actor is familiar with. I didn't mention the neighborhood's tall Washington palm trees captured in his Walter Mosley film, *Devil in a Blue Dress*. Or that *Training Day* for which he won an Oscar for Best Actor was filmed in that same Crenshaw neighborhood. Most significantly, I resisted the temptation to mention that the chef/owner of his favorite L.A. restaurant once prepared *pain chocolat*—a flakey French pastry filled with melted chocolate—in our kitchen when Kit and I lived at Breakfast Creek.

Of all the conversations I did NOT have with Denzel Washington that rainy Sundance night, the story of Suzanne Goin's *pain chocolat* is the story he would have loved most. Denzel is an accomplished cook himself, loves French cuisine and frequents Suzanne's popular restaurant, Lucques—cited recently in *The Week* magazine as L.A.'s best. Suzanne prepares a simple daily menu with fresh fish, seasonal organic produce and grass-fed meat raised by local farmers. But what makes her meals unique is her blend of classical French training, an apprenticeship with Alice Waters at Berkeley's Chez Panisse, and the Sundays she cooked alongside her father in her family's kitchen while growing up in the Hollywood Hills of Los Angeles.

While sipping a glass of wine between documentaries during Columbia's Fifth Annual True/False Filmfest this weekend, I momentarily let my mind drift back to the Sundance Institute where a tall woman and Denzel Washington are looking out at the rain. A nearby cameraman focuses and frames the image. Then, breaking the silence, a directive comes. "Quiet on the set. Lights. Camera. Action!"

Denzel turns to the woman, intrigued that she has not seized the opportunity to begin a conversation. "Are you involved in one of the institute workshops?" he asks.

"No," she answers, "I'm here because I want to be a writer."

"So tell me a story," the actor responds, flashing his famous killer smile.

"My story," the woman begins, "is about a young woman who grows up helping her father prepare the family's Sunday dinner. For a high school summer project, she finagles a job in the kitchen of L.A.'s most famous French restaurant, and then replaces the pastry chef who unexpectedly quits. While attending Brown University, she cooks on weekends at Providence's enormously popular Al Forno Restaurant. She also meets another Angelino studying at Brown, and the two make plans for their junior year abroad—Suzanne in London, Hayden in Rome."

"Sounds like a romance," the actor remarks.

"It was," the woman notes, "but a poignant one. They fall in love and marry, but her passion for a career in cooking and his for architecture get in the way. But before the couple split, they travel to Missouri where she prepares *pain chocolat* for his parents at a place in the country called Breakfast Creek. Suzanne's buttery creation was pure magic.

"The young architect ends up in Madrid working for Rafael Moneo—the Pritzker Award-winning Spanish architect who designed the new L.A. Cathedral. He eventually remarries and has three beautiful children. The beautiful chef returns to California, opens her own restaurant in L.A., marries a chef, writes a cookbook that wins the coveted James Beard Cookbook Award and then has twins."

Denzel looks intently at the woman who has described herself as a writer. The rain has nearly stopped. A few other actors who've been waiting on the sheltered porch start up the pathway that leads to the institute's hillside guest lodges. Taking her arm, Denzel and the woman walk at a comfortable pace, distancing themselves from the voices up ahead.

"Suzanne Goin made *pain chocolat* in your kitchen?" the actor asks after connecting the threads of the writer's culinary tale to the woman walking beside him. "In Missouri, you say?"

"True or False?" she answers with a hint of mischief. "You tell me."

Then, flashing a smile to die for and large enough to fill a movie screen, Denzel Washington turns, kisses the writer's hand and walks off into the night.... (2008)

✤ ✤ ✤

Printed in the United States
137273LV00004B/5/P